DIFFERENT FOR GIRLS

DIFFERENT FOR GIRLS

How Culture Creates Women

JOAN SMITH

Chatto & Windus
London

Published by Chatto & Windus 1997

2 4 6 8 10 9 7 5 3 1

First published in Great Britain in 1997 by
Chatto & Windus
Random House, 20 Vauxhall Bridge Road,
London SW1V 2SA

Random House Australia (Pty) Limited
20 Alfred Street, Milsons Point, Sydney,
New South Wales 2061, Australia

Random House New Zealand Limited
18 Poland Road, Glenfield,
Auckland 10, New Zealand

Random House South Africa (Pty) Limited
Endulini, 5A Jubilee Road, Parktown 2193, South Africa

Random House UK Limited Reg. No. 954009

A CIP catalogue record for this book
is available from the British Library

ISBN 0 701 16512 X

Papers used by Random House UK Limited are natural,
recyclable products made from wood grown in sustainable forests.
The manufacturing processes conform to the environmental
regulations of the country of origin.

Typeset by Palimpsest Book Production Limited,
Polmont, Stirlingshire
Printed and bound in Great Britain by
Mackays of Chatham PLC, Chatham, Kent

Don't you know that it's different for girls?
You're all the same . . .

Joe Jackson

Contents

Introduction

WHAT KIND OF women fascinate us at the end of the twentieth century? Diana, Princess of Wales, still seems to be the number one pin-up on both sides of the Atlantic, closely followed by Jackie Kennedy and Marilyn Monroe. No contemporary actress exudes star quality like Monroe, not even high earners like Sharon Stone or Demi Moore, whose careers remain dependent, as Marilyn's never was, on their most recent performance at the box-office. Jackie Kennedy's status has if anything risen since her death, with the Camelot myth continuing to inspire dozens of newspaper stories, magazine articles and books as the protagonists recede into a past recent enough for many of us to recall but far enough away to be bathed in a rosy nostalgic glow. What does it tell us about ourselves, however, if two of the women we most admire are dead and all three are linked with tragedy in its various guises: suicide, assassination, a desperately unhappy marriage?

That question can best be answered in the context of a spate of recent news stories with headlines like 'Assertive women "make men impotent"' (*Guardian*), 'Official: men finally losing the sex war' (*Sunday Times*), 'Taller and wider women match men at arrogance' (*Sunday Telegraph*). There are many, many more, and plenty of personal pieces on the feature pages of newspapers in which columnists agonise over the way in which the difference between men and women is being eroded. The ends of centuries are often periods of 'sexual anarchy', to borrow the phrase coined by the Victorian novelist George Gissing to describe his own *fin de siècle*, and ours is no exception. Every aspect of the relationship between men and women is being anxiously scrutinised, with commentators dividing between those who fear that we are becoming more alike than ever before, and pundits like John Aspinall, the right-wing maverick, who insisted in a recent article in the *Daily Telegraph* that 'the gap between the sexes ... can never be corrected'.

What these stories tend to have in common is rather less substance than is implied by the headlines. The *Sunday Times* article quoted above, for instance, refers to the fact that marginally more men than women, a paltry 820 to 803, complained about sex discrimination at work to the Equal Opportunities Commission in 1995 – more like a score draw than evidence that men have now overtaken women as the sex most discriminated against at work. What the story does reflect, however, is a widespread impression that if women are succeeding in any field, it must represent a loss to men. This is old-fashioned sex war stuff, made more piquant by a bit of *fin de siècle* panic, but it exposes an underlying anxiety which casts new light on our obsession with Diana, Marilyn and Jackie. Each of them, in her own way, represents a type of femininity which is both out-of-date and extremely seductive – for women as well as men – at a moment when the old certainties about gender no longer seem to apply. All three are soft, vulnerable and *sad*, so that we can admire them without feeling the envy that tougher, sassier women like Madonna inspire. They are also, in a world in which our attitudes to powerful women like Hillary Clinton and Cherie Blair are equivocal to say the least, the standard against which we are all measured – and measure ourselves – to some degree.

In that sense, there has seldom been a more exciting or a more confusing time to be a woman. We have made huge advances in employment, education, politics, and in our private lives, yet something still holds us back, and what that might be is the subject of this book. By focusing both on specific women and types – the *femme fatale*, the good wife, working mothers, women who choose not to have children – it examines the messages we get from our culture about female behaviour. Some of the chapters are relatively light in tone, others disturbingly dark; in the course of the book I move from an analysis of the kind of femininity espoused by the Princess of Wales to that tiny group of women who have broken the ultimate taboo, female murderers. How are they punished, the book asks, in comparison with men who commit murder? And what have we to learn from the cases of Myra Hindley and Rosemary West about our deepest fears on the nature of women?

Icons and ogres: these are the exemplars each culture uses to convey the boundaries that should not be crossed. How far can a woman go, at the end of the twentieth century, and still be counted a 'real' woman? Have we reached the point where a woman can act on her desires, sexual and otherwise, without fear of the consequences? Knowing that boundaries exist – and this book is an attempt to map them – is not an admission of defeat but an essential step in the process of redrawing them. In the 1990s, things still are, as the Joe Jackson song insists, different for girls. But I also want to show how close we have come, as mature women, to changing them.

Many people helped in different ways while I was researching and writing this book, and I would like to thank Alison Gorringe, Caroline Coon, Mark Bostridge, Lelia Green, Barbra Evans, Lyndall Gordon, David May, Jennifer Silverstone, Deborah Rogers, Kieran Prendiville, Lee Chester, James Maloney, Andrea Michell, David Miller, Sara Holloway and Jonathan Burnham. Its shape and many of its theories developed during long conversations with Anita Bennett, Bridget Rosewell and Maureen Freely, and it is to them, with affection and gratitude, that I dedicate *Different for Girls*.

Joan Smith
London, March 1997

Acknowledgements

The author and publishers would like to thank the Society of Authors as the Literary Representative of the Estate of John Masefield for permission to reproduce an extract from 'C.L.M.' by John Masefield. Every effort has been made to trace the owners of copyright material. Any omissions can be rectified in future editions.

Part I

Dreams of Fair Women

To Di For: *the Queen of Broken Hearts*

SHE GLIDED INTO the room on the arm of Sir John Kerr, British ambassador to Washington, who escorted her to the event in his Rolls Royce. The city's glitterati, and a contingent from New York, strained to get a glimpse of her as journalists swarmed round, noting every detail of her figure-hugging outfit. At a function where the kind of little black dress worn by Anna Wintour, British editor of American *Vogue*, is virtually *de rigueur* for women under a certain age, she confounded expectations by appearing in bridal white, a halter-necked gown of re-embroidered ribbon lace by the British designer Catherine Walker. Her hair a sleek blonde cap, diamonds glittering in her ears and on both wrists, she chatted easily to the other guests, obviously enjoying herself. As she talked, gripping a white clutch bag, her sapphire and diamond engagement ring sparkled on the third finger of her left hand.

Doe-eyed and smiling, the undisputed belle of the ball, she helped Katharine Graham, chairman of the *Washington Post* and host of the charity gala, greet celebrity guests like Elizabeth Dole, wife of the Republican party presidential candidate. In her shy, still hesitant public speaking voice, she charmed her audience with a short speech about research into breast cancer and read aloud some lines by the Australian poet Adam Lindsay Gordon which she had apparently chosen herself:

> Life is mostly froth and bubble,
> Two things stand like stone:
> Kindness in another's trouble,
> Courage in your own.

3

During dinner she shared a table with media stars like ABC's Barbara Walters before taking to the floor and dancing with the former chairman of the Joint Chiefs of Staff General Colin Powell and the fashion designers Oscar De La Renta and Calvin Klein. In a tribute to her own courage in overcoming the disaster of her failed marriage to the Prince of Wales, the orchestra played 'I Will Survive', the Gloria Gaynor song which, since it was released in the late 1970s, has become the anthem of deserted wives and girlfriends the world over. Tactfully, however, she left the floor at this point. 'She had no need to emphasise', gushed one report, 'what was plain for all to see – going solo has made her even stronger.'

'US dazzled by dancing Princess,' the *Daily Telegraph* noted in a half-page spread devoted to the event, with no fewer than three colour photographs, the following morning. The ball was widely regarded as a triumph, raising money for cancer research as well as demonstrating the unprecedented popularity of Diana, Princess of Wales, in the United States. Yet, like most events at which she is guest of honour, there was also something disturbingly off-key about it. First there was the unthinking adulation of other celebrities like the supermodel Naomi Campbell, who flew to Washington from London just for the event, announcing: 'I'm a total Diana fan. I'm only staying five hours.' Then there was the reverence universally accorded to the Princess, even though her chief public utterance consisted of a verse which could just as easily have graced a mass-produced get-well card. Finally there was the muted air of congratulation, as though the rich and famous had gathered not to greet a semi-detached member of the British royal family but to pay tribute to the survivor of some terrible ordeal – a train crash or massacre, say – who was only now venturing out in public after months of painful recuperation.

This was precisely the approach taken by *Hello!* magazine a few days later when it headlined its seven-page report of her supposedly private trip with the claim on its cover that 'Princess Diana is hailed in Washington as a true survivor'. Even in America, it seemed, audiences had responded with that sickly combination of awe, admiration and pity which has become the automatic reaction in recent years to any sighting of the Princess, whether in the flesh or in newspapers and magazines. This is especially true of those specialist publications, *Royalty* and *Majesty*, whose favourite cover girl she has long been. Features along the lines of 'The New Diana: How the Princess of Wales is finding the strength to transform her life' are their stock-in-trade, borrowing extensively from the vocabulary of trauma and survival to characterise her as a woman who has 'suffered great losses' and still endures 'bouts of self-doubt and depression'. Her grievances are rehearsed in their pages as faithfully as if she had dictated them herself: 'the Princess believes that she does not have a single supporter at Buckingham Palace' is a typical sentence from an article in *Royalty*. This interpretation of her situation, post-divorce, raises relatively few eyebrows; so accustomed have we all become to the notion of Diana as the plucky Princess, battling to overcome rejection by her husband and his family, not to mention the loss of her youthful hopes, that her increasing resemblance to one of the most baleful female characters in Victorian fiction has gone unnoticed. Yet her appearance in Washington in her virginal – and highly unfashionable – white gown merely served to underline it, especially as the pictures appeared in an issue of *Hello!* which also featured photographs of Eva Herzigova at her wedding to Bon Jovi drummer Tico Torres, in which the Czech supermodel sported a white lace dress whose silhouette was nearly identical to Diana's Catherine Walker outfit; neither woman would have looked out of place in *Brides* magazine. Here, from the novel, is the scene where the Princess's sinister *Doppelgänger* makes her first appearance:

> She was dressed in rich materials – satins, and lace, and silks – all of white. Her shoes were white. And she had a long white veil dependent from her hair, and she had bridal flowers in her hair, but her hair was white. Some bright jewels sparkled on her neck and on her hands, and some other jewels lay sparkling on the table.

The Princess of Wales is more smartly turned out than Miss Havisham, the jilted bride who presides like a vengeful ghost over the other characters in *Great Expectations*, but she gives every sense, like her fictional counterpart, of being a woman wedded to her unhappy past. Miss Havisham's attachment is more literal, frozen in the hour and place where her rejection occurred; both her watch and the clock in her darkened dressing-room are stopped at twenty minutes to nine, the precise moment when the news that her fiancé had jilted her came through. But Diana's bonds are almost as strong. Still housed, in the months after her divorce, in a wing of a residence, Kensington Palace, which belongs to her ex-husband's family (and which is home to several of his relatives, including Prince and Princess Michael of Kent); still using a version of his name and title; still living off his money, in the form of her divorce settlement; still doing the unpaid charity work, as much of it as suits her newly relaxed schedule, which has long been the genteel occupation of upper-middle-class wives; it is hardly, to quote the title of Andrew Morton's revised edition of his biography of the Princess of Wales, *Diana: Her New Life*. It would be more accurate to describe it as a scaled-down version of the unsatisfactory old one, with the additional discontents of an ambiguous public position to maintain – a title but no more curtsies, for example – and the spectacle of her ex-husband making ham-fisted attempts to persuade his future subjects to accept his longtime mistress. The Princess could detach herself more decisively from the Windsors but she does not, avoiding at all costs severing the connections, no matter how painful, which tie her to the royal family. If she seriously aspired to the independence for which magazines like *Hello!* have recently praised her, she could easily issue a statement along the following lines, perhaps tacking it to the railings of Buckingham Palace herself in a last symbolic gesture:

It has been announced that Diana, Princess of Wales, is to move shortly from Kensington Palace into a new home in London. Her sons, the Princes William and Harry, will continue to attend their respective boarding schools but will visit her regularly during the holidays. The Princess's plans, which she hopes to keep private, include finding a full-time job which will utilise her very special talents. To this end, she is reverting to her maiden name and, as befits a private citizen, will be known in future simply as Diana Spencer. Ms

Spencer hopes that the media, especially photographers, will respect her voluntary withdrawal from the public arena and leave her to get on with her life as a single woman.

Something of the sort, on a much smaller scale, is what many recently divorced women do. The house may be less spacious than the marital home, or rented, perhaps even a flat. The children probably live at home with their mother, and it's likely that she already has a job, full- or part-time. Her original surname, discarded ten or fifteen years ago without a second thought, suddenly becomes a far more attractive proposition than one belonging to a man she no longer likes – and who, judging by his actions, is planning to bestow it on someone else if he can square it with children, friends and family. (Who in her right mind wants to share a name and title with *the other woman*?) This is the reality, post-divorce, for most ex-wives in the 1990s: retrench, relocate, reorganise and, once the initial shock is over, find new purpose and a less stressful existence. The Princess, however, has openly rejected such a course, preferring to fill her life with visits to the gym, her therapist Susie Orbach and holidays with her children and women friends. Denied the vaguely defined ambassadorial role she aspired to in the run-up to her divorce, she is visibly at a loose end, drifting from one photo opportunity to the next, posing happily for the cameras when it pleases her and complaining of harassment when it doesn't and, on one occasion, enlisting a complete stranger to snatch film on her behalf.

So locked is she into her old life that we may even, if she and her ex-husband continue on the paths they have chosen, arrive at the bizarre situation of having two Princesses at the same time, giving rise to all sorts of confusion among people not sufficiently initiated to spot the small but significant difference between 'Diana, Princess of Wales', and 'the Princess of Wales'. There is a time-honoured test, involving peas and mattresses, for sorting out a *real* Princess from an impostor, but the tabloids, unable to fall back on this option, might well apply cruder criteria. (Diana, more photogenic than her rival Camilla Parker Bowles and trailing a long-standing reputation as one of the world's most beautiful women, looks set to win this round hands down.) But this is far from being the only contest she remains embroiled in. Her marriage reached its formal conclusion some time ago, but the custody battle goes on, not just for the loyalty of children and friends but for the affection of some fifty-five million people.

The stakes are high but Diana has devastating weapons in her armoury. The most striking feature of the television interview she gave to the BBC's *Panorama* programme in November 1995 was the way she chose to dress, in sombre dark blue and the kind of heavy make-up – thick eye-liner, as though to disguise eyes that had been weeping – which might be worn by someone in mourning. Even her hair, which usually testifies to the recent attentions of the world's most fashionable hairdressers, had the washed-out look of someone with far too much on her mind to worry about such trivialities. Placing herself in direct competition with her then mother-in-law, whose annual Christmas broadcasts are triumphantly devoid of all content other than as a reminder of the monarchy's continuing power to command our attention, the Princess provided an abundance of material which relegated world events to the inside pages of newspapers, not just in Britain but across several continents, for several days. Instead of platitudes about the royal family and the Commonwealth, delivered in flat tones by a woman whose appearance suggests she has just slipped indoors for tea after walking her dogs on a crisp winter afternoon, the Princess looked and sounded drained, like a crime victim who had been persuaded by the police to meet the press and talk about her ordeal. The story she poured out could scarcely have been more dramatic, involving deception, betrayal and despair in the very highest circles, but there was no need simply to take her word for it; what she was asking, in effect, was that people should trust the evidence of their own eyes. Those very viewers who remembered her as a glowing girl, descending like Cinderella from her glass coach on the day of her wedding in 1981, could see for themselves that she had been transformed by her marriage into this haggard, slightly dishevelled, rigidly controlled young woman. They would be distressed, but not astonished, by the following exchange:

'Do you know what I touch here?' she said, laying her hands, one upon the other, on her left side.

'Yes, ma'am.'
'What do I touch?'
'Your heart.'
'Broken!'

In fact it's Miss Havisham speaking to Pip, not the Princess to Martin Bashir, but the message of her *Panorama* programme was much the same. Innocence had turned to bitter experience as the world fell in love with fresh, innocent Lady Diana Spencer; the world but, as it turned out, not her husband. Now he and his family were trying, behind the scenes, to dislodge her from that place in the people's affections to which she felt entitled. But she would not go quietly. She would fight for her right, not to the throne as the Prince of Wales's consort, but to an unconstitutional position which was not in his gift, thus completing the metamorphosis he had initiated fourteen years before – radiant bride to jilted wife – on her own terms. Prince Charles could prevent her formal coronation in Westminster Abbey at some unknown and, given his mother's robust health, possibly distant date in the future. But he could not stop her reigning, in her own words, as the queen of hearts. Broken or otherwise.

A few weeks later, when Princess Diana was photographed at a hospital in green theatre cap and gown, observing open heart surgery, plenty of people wondered aloud whether she was taking this conceit rather too literally. Yet if the Princess was still trying, figuratively or otherwise, to inhabit a fairy tale, her husband's reading of their joint history had already revealed another kind of pretension. Their marriage, he told his biographer Jonathan Dimbleby, resembled a Greek tragedy, thus comparing his own fate to the disasters which befell archetypal heroes like Oedipus, Agamemnon and Orestes. The analogy was far from exact; it is hard to recall any extant Athenian drama in which a weak-willed prince is pushed into a dynastic marriage by his overbearing father, only to watch in irritable dismay as his young bride descends into tears and bulimia. *Carolus Rex* it is not, for which the Prince of Wales should be eternally grateful: the wronged heroines of Sophocles, Aeschylus and Euripides, often queens or princesses whose husbands or lovers have abandoned them for other women, favoured more drastic forms of revenge than talking to the contemporary equivalent of Andrew Morton, hacking at their wrists with a lemon slicer and throwing themselves at glass-fronted cabinets. Clytemnestra, enraged by her husband's adultery with his Trojan captive Cassandra, murdered him with the connivance of her lover Orestes. Phaedra fell in love with her stepson Hippolytus and hounded him to his death when he rejected her. Medea, deserted by her lover Jason, killed her rival with a poisoned robe and butchered her children. The point about Greek tragedy is that it is the original genre of which it might accurately be said that 'no one gets out of here alive'.

Diana's spiteful (and apparently libellous) remark at a Christmas party in 1995 to Tiggy Legge-Bourke, the nanny employed by Prince Charles, is hardly in the same league for venom. But her carefully cultivated public persona suggests her awareness that the words 'tragic' and 'queen' have an ancient affinity which she is happy to exploit. The would-be queen of hearts *said* on television that she was a strong woman who had survived a loveless marriage and overcome a debilitating illness, but she also talked about the way she had been deceived by her husband, let down by the lover she adored, and denied the special destiny which, according to Andrew Morton at least, she had always believed to be in store for her. ('I knew I had to keep myself tidy for what lay ahead' is her explanation, in *Diana: Her True Story*, for hanging on to her virginity until her marriage.) This was someone, in other words, to whom terrible things had been done and whose statement 'I am strong' was contradicted at every turn by language and visual cues which insisted 'I am a victim'. The message was that she had been maltreated by her husband, by the Queen, by unnamed staff at Buckingham Palace, and by Captain James Hewitt. (It is worth mentioning here that this presentation of her relationship with the former army officer might have been calculated on her part as well as reflecting a genuine sense of grievance. Publicly admitting to adultery is a dangerous ploy, as Prince Charles learned to his cost after his candid TV interview with Jonathan Dimbleby the previous summer. Diana, or her advisers, probably recognised the Hewitt episode as the trickiest area of her encounter with Bashir

– the only section, in fact, in which she risked alienating even her most committed supporters. The tactic, if it was one, was conspicuously successful. Reactions to the Princess's confession were muted, in stark contrast to the calumny heaped on the Duchess of York a year later when the *Sun* rehashed old material about two affairs under the vicious headlines 'Broken: Fergie's final shame' and 'Fergie takes flight: £4 million in debt, shamed as adulteress'.)

The rider that she had been very much in love with Hewitt, and that the affair had made her unhappy, placed Diana's admission in the context of a series of betrayals: even if it cast doubt on her judgement of men, what was the unhappy Princess guilty of other than loving not wisely but too well? And was it really surprising that a guileless young woman, whose growing up was done under relentless public scrutiny and without much support from her older, supposedly more mature husband, should make the same mistake twice? Blame for her affair with Hewitt was thus laid at the door of her neglectful spouse – one cad leads to another, so to speak – while, as if to reinforce her claim that she was the victim of a continuing conspiracy by Prince Charles and his friends, the junior minister Nicholas Soames obligingly went on television the very same evening and questioned the Princess's sanity. This breathtaking piece of idiocy on the part of one of the Prince's cronies earned Soames an implied rebuke from John Major, who hurried to distance himself and his already unpopular party from an outburst which was widely considered to be in bad taste. More to the point, it demonstrated how badly the Prince's supporters had misjudged the impact of Diana's performance. The *Panorama* interview was much more than a blatantly partisan account of her marriage; it marked her invention, at a stroke, of a new and multi-faceted identity for herself. Appropriating the language of such disparate discourses as traditional romance, psychotherapy and even feminism, she had succeeded in reaching out to the broadest of all possible constituencies – so much so that the then *Guardian* columnist Suzanne Moore rushed into print hailing the Princess, however improbably, as a heroine for the women's movement. (Moore's near-canonisation of Diana, interspersed with lines from 'I Will Survive', may have been the first time she was publicly linked with the Gaynor song. The *Guardian* has much to answer for on this score.)

Suzanne Moore was not alone in her enthusiasm for the Princess's performance. Anyone who had ever been jilted or endured an unhappy love affair, which is to say the entire population over the age of fourteen with the exception of a handful of celibates and cynics, understood, empathised and felt for her. No longer just a spoiled and unstable young woman with an expensive taste in clothes, she had exploited the directness and immediacy of television to outflank her enemies and re-create herself as the archetypal wronged woman. She was *la traviata* personified, a latter-day *dame aux caméllias*, Anna Karenina after Vronsky abandoned her. No wonder she dressed in *faux* mourning as she got ready, at Kensington Palace, for her appearance before the TV cameras; she had quite literally, one might say, got the blues. But by the time the time the credits rolled, she did at least have the consolation of knowing that millions of people had got them with her.

What Diana seemed to have forgotten, and most people were too dazzled by her performance to recall, was the traditional fate of the women with whom she had chosen to bracket herself. Clytemnestra, Medea, Phaedra, Sophonisba, Dido, Lucretia, Desdemona, Madame Butterfly, Violetta, Norma, Mimi, even twentieth-century heroines like Maria from *West Side Story*: they all wind up young, beautiful and dead. Poison, strangulation, speeding trains, tuberculosis, above all self-inflicted wounds, these are what lie in wait for the *donna abbandonata*; it is emphatically not a long-term career option. Diana's own suicide attempts during her marriage, according to Andrew Morton who first documented them, were 'cries for help' rather than concerted efforts to kill herself. But what the biography did reveal was a depressive strain to the Princess's character which manifested itself not in a serious suicide bid but, beginning with the week of her wedding, in a series of tearful temporary collapses. Here, chosen virtually at random, are some typical sentences from Morton's book:

- The public glimpsed her frustration and desperation the

weekend before the wedding when she left a polo field at Tidworth in floods of tears.

- As soon as the camera lights were switched on, it triggered the churning emotions in her heart and she broke down and wept uncontrollably.

- . . . a few hours earlier she had collapsed in paroxysms of tears and seriously considered calling [the wedding] off.

- Behind closed doors Diana cried her eyes out with nervous exhaustion.

- The sound of voices raised in anger and hysterical sobbing could be plainly heard coming from the suite of rooms occupied by the Prince and Princess of Wales.

- She was often in tears as they travelled to the various venues, telling her husband that she simply could not face the crowds.

- When she returned to the penthouse suite they occupied in the Pan Pacific hotel overlooking Vancouver Bay, Diana flopped down and sobbed her eyes out.

- She was weepy and nervy, anxious about her baby . . . while neglecting herself.

- Diana was in tears when she saw the picture in Monday's papers.

- There were still tears and traumas but the worst was over.

- Diana burst into tears, overwhelmed by the show of affection from waiting well-wishers . . .

The biography, and its serialisation in the *Sunday Times* in 1992, were universally believed to have the Princess's imprimatur. It is reasonable to assume not just that its lachrymose portrait of Diana is accurate but that, more to the point, this is how she *wanted* to be seen: as a fragile, pitiable figure rather than a poised young woman of thirty-one, her age when the book was published. In addition, many of the remarks attributed by Morton to Diana – 'The night before the wedding I was very calm, deathly calm. I felt I was the lamb to the slaughter' – are consistent with the appearance she has given elsewhere of clinging to, even of embracing, her victim status. It is far from unusual for the Princess to weep in public, and the frequency with which she has been pictured in this state in newspapers and magazines suggests, if not some form of collusion, at least that editors have accepted her version of her life story – the Princess of Wails – at face value. Yet, looked at objectively, it is hard to resist two conclusions: that Diana is self-deluding in her assessment of her own situation, and that she has been astonishingly successful in persuading vast numbers of people to collude in that deception.

What, after all, has happened to her? An unworldly nineteen-year-old when the Prince of Wales proposed to her, it is understandable that she did not immediately see the warning signs – or, as the apprehensions she later expressed in Andrew Morton's book suggest, that she chose to ignore them. 'While a small voice inside her head', according to Morton, 'told her that she would never become queen but would have a tough life [,] she found herself accepting his offer and telling him repeatedly how much she loved him.' Yet she went ahead with her marriage to a sexually experienced older man she barely knew, whose temper and inclinations might have been gauged from his insistence, until their engagement, that she address him as 'Sir'. Nor can she have been unaware that his family was one of the most conventional and self-servingly dynastic in the country. Its subsequent closing of ranks against her, no matter how reprehensible, was entirely predictable; those critics who argue that there is something wrong with an institution that has no place for a woman as gifted as the Princess of Wales have simply mistaken its nature ('Royal family arbitrary and undemocratic' is not, after all, much of a headline). Her divorce settlement, said to be in the region of £17 million, is not ungenerous compared to the sums that many ex-wives have to live on – especially in marriages where their personal financial contribution, like Diana's, has been nil. Her chief ground for complaint, in the final analysis, is the old one that she has been denied her rightful role in a fairy tale, even though it has long since been demonstrated that, even as the crowds turned out to cheer the happy couple on their way to St Paul's Cathedral on 29 July 1981, the protagonists themselves were already having doubts about the wisdom of what they were doing. The Prince's ambiguity was audible in his evasive answer, during a TV interview just after his engagement, to a question about whether he was in love: 'Whatever love means.' Diana's own doubts, and her suspicions about her husband-to-be's relationship with Camilla Parker Bowles, are documented in Morton's book. Even the prelate who married them, Robert Runcie, then Archbishop of Canterbury, later confessed his misgivings about the couple's compatibility to his biographer, Humphrey Carpenter.

Is this the stuff of tragedy, or a series of bad judgements? Has Diana, with two sons she obviously adores and reasonably comfortable circumstances, really come out of it so badly? Why does her popularity soar each time some new mishap, no matter how minor, befalls her and is splashed all over the tabloid press? It is as if the Princess, having decided to make a career out of her unhappiness, needs to remind her public from time to time of all the wrongs that have been heaped upon her – and her admirers have grown accustomed to responding, like Pavlovian dogs, with the sympathy and indignation on which she depends. Yet it is doubtful whether the affection even of millions of anonymous people can ever make up for the wounds inflicted during her marriage – or, more importantly, for those she acquired in her childhood, when her parents' marriage broke down and they separated. Morton's biography records this significant moment, when Diana was only six years old, and the feelings of abandonment which seem to have been her constant companion ever since:

She could hear her father loading suitcases into the boot of a car, then Frances, her mother, crunching across the gravel forecourt, the clunk of the car door being shut and the sound of a car engine revving and then slowly fading as her mother drove through the gates of Park House and out of her life ... A quarter of a century later, it is a moment she can still picture in her mind's eye and she can still summon up

15

the painful feelings of rejection, breach of trust and isolation that the break-up of her parents' marriage signified to her.

Lonely children frequently console themselves with fantasies in which they are heroes and heroines, a resource so sustaining to them that they develop an ability to draw others into their games. When Lady Diana Spencer got engaged to the Prince of Wales she became a focus for other people's dreams and visions, embodying the age-old fairy story about the commoner who captures the heart of a prince. It was not so obvious at the time that the process was a two-way street, that the price we would pay for imposing our fantasies on her slender form was to absorb hers in return, no matter how distorted a version of events they would turn out to represent. Yet that is precisely what has happened to millions of people in Britain, Europe, the United States and across the world; in the aftermath of the Princess's divorce, we have become so used to feeling sorry for her and admiring her courage that reality is never allowed to intrude. As a consequence, the perils of the course she has embarked upon have not been fully set out, obvious though they are to a detached observer. Here, from *Great Expectations*, is the moment when Pip glimpses the grim truth behind Miss Havisham's festive white gown:

> It was not in the first few moments that I saw all these things, though I saw more of them in the first moments than might be supposed. But, I saw that everything within my view which ought to be white, had been white long ago, and had lost its lustre, and was faded and yellow. I saw that the bride within the bridal dress had withered like the dress, and like the flowers, and had no brightness left but the brightness of her sunken eyes. I saw that the dress had been put upon the rounded figure of a young woman, and that the figure upon which it now hung loose, had shrunk to skin and bone.

This, graphically described, is the fate which threatens the *donna abbandonata* who refuses to expire gracefully at the end of the final act. For the moment, Diana's choice is between personal happiness and the charisma that attaches to her as a young, glamorous and wronged woman. As she gets older, the choice will become more stark. One day in the not too distant future, it may occur to her that the part she has embraced so enthusiastically since the breakdown of her marriage is leading nowhere, except to more tears and loneliness. Her public likes her this way, no question, but is it a role she is prepared to die for?

Good Wives

WHEN HER ELDEST sister, Meg, falls in love towards the end of *Little Women*, tomboyish Jo March is horrified. 'I knew there was mischief brewing,' she exclaims; 'I felt it; and now it's worse than I imagined. I just wish I could marry Meg myself, and keep her safe in the family.' Jo's outspoken onslaughts on her sister's suitor John Brooke are presented by Louisa May Alcott as tragicomic, the natural reaction of a rebellious teenager who does not yet understand the attraction between mature men and women. It is the product of an innocence which the other characters find engaging and infuriating by turns. Convinced she has persuaded Meg to reject Brooke, Jo is all the more dismayed when, entering the parlour where she thinks her sister has finally dismissed the man she sees as her rival, she finds instead a scene of total capitulation:

> Going in to exult over a fallen enemy, and to praise a strong-minded sister for the banishment of an objectionable lover, it certainly *was* a shock to behold the aforesaid enemy sitting serenely on the sofa, with the strong-minded sister enthroned upon his knee, and wearing an expression of the most abject submission. Jo gave a sort of gasp, as if a cold shower-bath had suddenly fallen upon her – for such an unexpected turning of the tables actually took her breath away.

The blow Jo has sustained is not just a reaction to the successful invasion of the sisters' feminine world by an outsider. It is also a realisation of the power of male sexuality and of the inevitability of Meg's surrender to it, with the likelihood of her own future capitulation also implied. In a novel which has explicit parallels with Bunyan's *Pilgrim's Progress*, Alcott suggests that this is Jo's particular burden as a high-spirited girl to whom such acquiescence is, for the moment at least, unthinkable; it is nevertheless a woman's Christian duty to marry and, at the end of the novel, Jo's friend Laurie – literally the boy next door – tries to console her with the thought that 'it will be very jolly to see Meg in her own little house'.

There is something childish about the image, as though Alcott has unwittingly visualised Meg, in keeping with the book's title, in a doll's house rather than a grown woman's home. At the same time, the phrase she uses to describe Meg's posture as she supposedly crosses the threshold into adulthood – 'abject submission' – indicates a considerable degree of ambiguity on her part. Is this how Alcott, a feminist of sorts who never married, unconsciously viewed the state of matrimony? There are tensions in *Little Women* between the March girls' good-natured (on the whole) acceptance of a woman's fate and an underlying unease, expressed in the text in the form of Jo's frequent and vociferous rebellions against it. But the novel's overt message is that they will one day become the *Good Wives* of its much less iconic sequel. (Liminal states, which is where *Little Women* leaves Meg and her sisters, are far more intriguing than the certainties of adult life. This was especially the case in the second half of the nineteenth century, when the options open to women were only just beginning to expand.)

Since *Little Women* was published in 1868, much has changed – not least the fact that huge numbers of marriages now finish in divorce in Western Europe and North America. In the novel, which is set against the background of the American Civil War, the girls' father, an army chaplain, is unavoidably absent until the final pages, when he and his wife are reunited to rediscover 'the first chapter of the romance which for them began some twenty years ago'. Alcott's assumption is that only death, from old age or through some calamity such as war or illness, can sever the marriage bond. Nowadays, however, divorce is just as likely as death to terminate relationships. In the United States, half of all marriages end this way; in Britain, the figure is 40 per cent, the highest rate of breakdown in Europe. The number of divorces in Britain has risen inexorably from an insignificant 6,092 in 1938 to an annual figure in excess of 150,000 in the early Nineties, peaking at 162,579 in 1993 (in 1994, the latest year for which figures are available at the time of writing, it was 158,200). And, for complex reasons which may well include publicity about the high rate of marital breakdown, there has been a corresponding drop in the popularity of marriage – in 1993, the figure fell below 300,000 in Britain for the first time in forty years. In 1994, it was down to 291,000, compared with 404,700 in 1971 – a drop of 28 per cent in just over twenty years.

This means that for every two British couples promising to stay together 'till death us do part', another is getting divorced – a situation which the Church of England, law officers, Conservative MPs and other establishment voices have come to regard as a crisis. Dr John Habgood, then Archbishop of York and the second most senior prelate in Britain, called on John Major's government, with its high-profile commitment to 'family values', to cut income tax for married couples; society had been 'sending the wrong message about the value which it attached to marriage', the Archbishop's office announced. 'The institution of marriage is beleaguered as never before,' *The Times* admitted in 1993, a state of affairs which persuaded its executives to commission a survey into attitudes to marriage and divorce. The results were confusing to say the least, the paper's tone suggesting that its journalists were trying to reassure themselves as much as their readers:

> Our investigations show that respect for marriage as a core national value still holds sway although this support is being eroded. Recession, unemployment, infidelity and the relative ease of obtaining a divorce frequently send couples to the lawyer's office.

Other newspapers, notably the *Daily Telegraph*, have been running regular anguished features along the lines of 'how children are damaged by divorce', but there is no single view on how the supposed crisis should be dealt with. 'All it takes is a little staying power,' an article in the *Mail on Sunday's* colour supplement announced briskly in April 1995. Blaming the problem on 'the first blooms of free love in the 1960s' and 'the divorce reform of the 70s' – Leo Abse's private member's bill actually became law in 1969 – *You* magazine concluded: 'Couples who have tunnelled through the hard times together and surfaced intact are often stronger and closer for it. Hanging on in through the heartaches can reap many rewards.' The *Sun*, which may have a surer grasp of its readers' sensibilities on this subject, made its own idiosyncratic contribution to the debate with a cheerful little guide entitled '20 ways to leave your lover: what happens when I Do becomes I'll Sue'. But *You* magazine's homily was in keeping with the widespread assumption that, even if nobody knows quite how to achieve it, persuading people to stay married is a far more desirable goal than questioning the relevance of an institution which, for significant numbers of people, simply isn't working.

More to the point, it isn't working for women. This dramatic reversal of conventional wisdom, which holds that women long to get married and men resist as long as they can, has not yet been fully absorbed; on the contrary Shaw's assertion, in *Man and Superman*, that 'it is a woman's business to get married as soon as possible, and a man's to keep unmarried as long as he can' has a tenacious hold on the popular imagination. In June 1995, when the former Beirut hostage John McCarthy announced that he had split up with his girlfriend, Jill Morrell, the story was almost universally reported in terms that assumed *Morrell* to be the disappointed partner. Indeed, the tabloids shared her supposed grief, reflecting the way in which, from the moment McCarthy was released from his long captivity in Lebanon, they had urged the couple to marry, sometimes behaving as though their readers were entitled to an engagement followed by a fairy-tale wedding. Morrell, plucky, blonde and determined, had led the campaign for McCarthy's release, putting pressure on the Foreign Office and using skilful PR tactics to make sure he was not forgotten; why couldn't he do the decent thing and lead her down the aisle? When Morrell and McCarthy finally split, journalists were as distraught as they assumed the no-longer-happy couple to be. 'They tried their best to make the romance work but sadly there is no happy ending,' one newspaper sermonised. 'The impression remains', wrote journalist Daniel McGrory, after speaking to 'one of the few friends to have genuinely shared their torment', that Jill Morrell 'would have married him tomorrow given the chance'. The general feeling was that the McCarthy–Morrell saga could have only one satisfactory outcome – the happy couple emerging from a country church to showers of confetti and a scrum of photographers and TV crews – and that the British public had somehow been cheated out of it.

The *Daily Telegraph*, one of the few newspapers to introduce a note of caution, suggested that 'a public insatiable for romance may have to accept that the couple who fought so hard to be together may now be happier apart'. For even if McCarthy and Morrell had satisfied the tabloids' sentimental longing for wedding bells, their chances of staying together would have been just a bit better than evens. And, if the marriage had broken down, the statistics suggest it would have been Morrell, not McCarthy, who initiated the break. In the ten years up to 1989, according to the Office of Population, Censuses and Surveys, around three-quarters of divorce proceedings were begun by women. This, in spite of the often disastrous financial consequences of divorce for the female partner in a marriage, has been the pattern for most of our century.

No one would discover this significant degree of disillusion on the part of women from reading any of the half-dozen British magazines devoted entirely to the subject of weddings. A typical issue of *Brides* magazine displays, on its cover, a photograph of a model clutching a bouquet of apricot roses to the white lace bodice of her traditional wedding gown (£2,900 from Bruce Oldfield Ready to Wear, which says something about the magazine's relationship to real life). Inside there are articles on 'the most beautiful dresses for a radiant bride' and 'how to solve last-minute wedding dilemmas'. The latter include the bizarre story of a woman who discovered, three days before her wedding, that her dressmaker had gone on holiday without delivering the bridesmaids' dresses *and promptly rang the police*; amazingly, they were unable to help. There is a nod in the direction of changing *mores*, in the shape of an article flagged on the cover as 'Why marry? Is living together enough?' Unsurprisingly, since the trend towards cohabitation threatens to put magazines like *Brides* out of business, it turns out to refer to a feature in which 'five couples say why living together wasn't enough'. One of them, Stella and Mark, cite religious reasons on her part – she was brought up a Roman Catholic – and pressure on his. 'It was never a secret', says Mark, 'that Stella wanted to marry me for a long time before I asked her.' Yet anecdotal evidence and surveys as well as statistics support the view that if this was ever true, if marriage used to be genuinely popular with women instead of a mostly unavoidable and therefore unexamined necessity, it is the case no longer. A typical poll, reported in the magazine *Men's Health* in June 1996, suggested that among a group of over-thirty-fives, married men with children had the 'highest life satisfaction' and their wives the lowest. The most contented women in the survey were single and childless, suggesting that what used to be called spinsterhood is far from the unmitigated disaster for women that it was once assumed to be.

Unfortunately, British governments and many MPs from all political parties continue to take as sentimental a view of marriage as *Brides* magazine. 'The institution of marriage should be supported. Where a marriage may have broken down the married couple should be encouraged to take all practical steps to save the marriage' was the opening proposition of the Family Law Bill published in April 1996, thus placing the outgoing Conservative government in the contortionist position of attempting to reform divorce law from a starting-point hostile to it. The 1996 act, passed on a free vote in the House of Commons, put an end to the quickie 'fault' divorce favoured by three out of four separating couples, implying that a majority of MPs shared the *Mail on Sunday*'s perspective on the problem: that the high divorce rate reflected a lack of staying power on the part of husbands and wives which could be rectified by a compulsory cooling-off period. But does anyone really believe that indifferent, angry or betrayed spouses will change their minds because they have to kick their heels for eighteen months before they can divorce, the qualifying period decided on by MPs? (The White Paper had suggested a less arduous twelve months.) That warring couples will be placated by mediation or being forced to sit through a video on the consequences of splitting up?

In effect, the new divorce law is an admission that governments are and will continue to be trapped by the sheer success, in terms of take-up, of the 1969 Divorce Reform Act. The number of divorces more than tripled in the following decade; much as MPs and ministers dislike the tangled family relationships which result from marital breakdown, and the cost to the state of legal aid and benefits to one-parent families, they are hardly going to court an extra dose of unpopularity by forcing thousands of voters to stay in unhappy marriages. Nor, given the highly publicised marital discords of Conservative MPs and former ministers like David Mellor, Alan Clark, Steven Norris and Tim Yeo, is the Conservative Party in any position to make a bid for the moral high ground. That has been left to austere commentators like Melanie Phillips of the *Observer*. Phillips overstated the case when she claimed that the marriage contract ceases to mean anything if you can get out of it, yet she was groping towards another, equally unpalatable truth. Put simply, there is only one sure-fire way of dramatically reducing the number of divorces, which is to make the whole procedure so daunting and expensive, not to mention socially suicidal, that almost no one but the truly desperate will attempt it.

This, as it happens, is a fairly precise description of the situation which existed in England and Wales before the passing of the second Divorce Reform Act in 1923. When divorce was made available in the civil courts in 1857, finally extending the option beyond the tiny circle of wealthy aristocrats who could afford the staggering expense of a parliamentary divorce, the terms were drawn so tightly that only a tiny minority of married couples were able to satisfy them: 141 in 1861, rising to the still negligible figure of 580 in 1911. Taken on their own, these statistics are sometimes used to suggest that the reign of Queen Victoria was the golden age of marriage – that they reflect the existence of a stable, non-divorcing society in which even those couples who discovered they were unsuited simply made the best of things. According to this analysis, people found a degree of satisfaction in doing their duty; the scapegoat for all our present woes is the rise of 'affective individualism', that insistence on a right to personal happiness which over rides other, more socially desirable imperatives like providing a secure environment in which children can grow up.

This superficially attractive theory has been comprehensively demolished by the work of Professor Lawrence Stone, until recently professor of history at Princeton University. Stone, whose research is informed by a liberal but not a radical perspective, is unequivocal in his condemnation of the situation of married women in England well into the nineteenth century. In his book *Road to Divorce*, he argues that a married woman 'was the nearest approximation in free society to a slave'. Specifically, he says:

> Her person, her property both real and personal, her earnings, and her children all passed on marriage into the absolute control of her husband. The latter could use her sexually as and when he wished, and beat her (within reason) or confine her for disobedience to any orders. The children were entirely at the disposal of the father, who was legally empowered to remove them, put them to work, or marry them, just as he thought fit, without consulting the wishes of his wife. He could even debar his wife from ever setting eyes on them or writing to them.

Stone's scholarly research on marriage represents a startling catalogue of the injustice done to married women by the English legal system. No wonder most wives were good; they had no choice, unless they were prepared to risk violence, coercion and social ostracism. The proposition that a husband could beat his wife with a stick no thicker than his thumb sounds apocryphal but dates back to a declaration by an English judge in 1782. The barbaric practice of kidnapping and locking up fugitive wives, although not frequently resorted to, was not outlawed until more than a century later, in 1891. Until 1839, a separated wife had no right of access to her children; an act of that year gave the courts limited rights to transfer custody of children under the age of seven to the mother, as long as she had not committed adultery. It took another eighteen years for a divorced or separated woman to be allowed custody of children up to the age of fourteen, still with the rider that she had to be the 'innocent' party.

As late as 1862, a judge remarked that 'it will probably have a salutary effect on the interests of public morality that it should be known that a woman, if guilty of adultery, will forfeit ... all right to the custody of or access to her children'. He said nothing about adulterous fathers, and it is clear that the fear of losing all contact with their children haunted Victorian wives and mothers. The Hollywood movie *Mrs Doubtfire*, in which Robin Williams dressed up in drag to get access to his children after a messy marriage breakdown, inverted a staple motif of mid-nineteenth-century fiction, namely the 'guilty' wife who returns in disguise as governess to her children or their friends. In Charlotte Brontë's novel *Shirley*, the heroine's governess 'Mrs Pryor' turns out to be the mother of her best friend, Caroline Helstone; her revelation of her real identity saves her daughter from near-fatal anorexic decline. A much more melodramatic treatment of the theme appears in Mrs Henry Wood's 1861 tear-jerker, *East Lynne*, in which the disgraced, disguised and disfigured Lady Isabel Vane is present at the deathbed of her own son without being able to tell him who she is. 'Lady – wife – mother!' Mrs Wood exhorted her female readers, 'should you ever be attempted to abandon your home ... bear unto death, rather than forfeit your fair name and your fair conscience.' (T. A. Palmer's stage version of the novel contained the famous phrase 'Dead! and ... never called me mother', which does not appear in the book.)

The situation was much the same in the United States, where the promise of domestic bliss held out to biddable wives was balanced by overt threats of disgrace if they stepped out of line. Daniel Wise, author of *The Young Lady's Counsellor*, summed up both options in a book dedicated 'to the young women of America' in 1851:

Everything has its appointed sphere, within which alone it can flourish. Men and women have theirs. They are not exceptions to this truth, but examples of it. To be happy and prosperous, they must abide in them. Man is fitted for the storms of public life, and, like the petrel, can be happy amidst their rudest surges. Woman is formed for the calm of home. She may venture, like the land-bird, to invade the sphere of man, but she will encounter storms which she is utterly unfitted to meet; happiness will forsake her breast, her own sex will despise her, men will be unable to love her, and when she dies she will fill an unhonored grave.

In England and Wales, an 'unhonored grave' was not the worst prospect an absconding wife might face. Until the first Married Women's Property Act was passed in 1870, after a struggle lasting nearly twenty years in both houses of parliament, married women stood to lose their property as well as their children if their marriages broke down. Cases cited by law reformers in the 1850s included that of a French milliner who set up a successful business in London, only to be ruined when her separated husband suddenly appeared, 'pounced upon her earnings, sold her stock in trade, carried off the proceeds, collected the debts, and returned with her entire fortune to Paris'. None of these rules on property, income or the custody of children applied to husbands, no matter how dreadful their behaviour. Indeed, for more than sixty years after divorce was legalised, a wife could not divorce her husband for adultery alone; she needed to be able to cite other grounds such as cruelty or desertion, whereas she could be ejected from her marriage for a single act of intercourse with another man. Throughout the nineteenth century, desperate women who tried to escape from miserable or violent unions had no guarantee of success, as is demonstrated by a remarkable case which came before the courts in 1835. In that year, a Mrs Belcher left her husband on the perfectly reasonable ground that he had just infected her with venereal disease for the third time in three years. Mr Belcher was so infuriated by his wife's flight that he launched an action for restitution of his conjugal rights, a legal device to force her return to his house. Mrs Belcher promptly responded with a demand for a legal separation on grounds of cruelty.

The judge hearing the case turned her down flat. Because Mr Belcher had contracted the disease before his marriage and not by committing adultery, he ruled that the repeated infections did not amount to cruelty; even worse, he granted Mr Belcher's request that his wife be ordered to live with him. Lawrence Stone, commenting on the case in *Road to Divorce*, observes that while the judge could not order Mrs Belcher into her husband's bed, marital rape was not a crime in 1835 and 'there was nothing to stop Belcher from taking his wife by force'.

It is a telling fact that this privilege, immunity from prosecution for marital rape, was removed from English and Welsh husbands only in 1991. Until then, following a ruling by a seventeenth-century judge, Sir Matthew Hale, the courts held that a woman gave perpetual consent to sex with her husband when she married and could not withdraw it. It took a vigorous, decade-long campaign in Britain to gain wide acceptance of the not particularly radical proposition that rape within marriage is as damaging as other types of non-consensual sex. In 1991, in an embarrassed judgment which characterised the existing situation, rather late in the day, as 'anachronistic and offensive', the law lords finally upheld a conviction for attempted rape where the parties involved were a husband and his estranged wife – and were promptly denounced in the *Spectator* for bowing to 'feminist orthodoxy'.

It is not only feminists, however, who have arrived at the conclusion that marriage was, for centuries, an asymmetrical liaison which regulated female conduct in a far more draconian manner than it did that of men. Lawrence Stone, for example, admits that marriages used to be held together by 'the overwhelming ideology of female subordination and inferiority, drilled into every member of the society by clerical sermons, state regulations, marital handbooks, and both elite and popular culture'. Viewed without the ameliorating prism of romance, traditional marriage emerges as a means of ensuring the orderly transmission of property and, crucially, of protecting husbands from the horror of 'spurious issue' – the introduction into the family unit, through the wife's infidelity, of another man's child. The skeletal remains of this harsh reality can occasionally be glimpsed behind the shimmering veil which descends, however inappropriately, on high-profile couples like the Prince and Princess of Wales; eyebrows were raised when one of Lady Diana Spencer's more candid relatives assured the world that the prince's chosen bride was a virgin, yet it is now clear that the marriage was made, on Charles's side, for dynastic rather than romantic reasons. She was in love, he needed an heir.

In that sense, the royal wedding exemplified, to an extreme degree, the confusion surrounding marriage in the final decades of the twentieth century. Is it a public declaration of love, valid only as long as both parties wish it to be; a preliminary step towards creating a stable environment for bringing up children; or an acceptance of the state's continuing interest in – and right to regulate – the private lives of its citizens? Diana, Princess of Wales, divorced wife of the heir to the throne, is in a unique and unenviable position: she is an anachronism, a poignant reminder of how much women stood to lose from failed marriages when the cards were stacked, as they remain in the case of the heir to the throne, in favour of husbands. For her, divorce has meant giving up a title (HRH), much of her status, and the prospect of being Queen. For the rest of us, such considerations do not apply, and a combination of circumstances – more women going out to work and the availability of state benefits – means that the financial penalties associated with divorce, although real, are no longer unbearably heavy.

Two trends are clear: a sizeable minority of couples have begun to work out ways of living which do not include formal marriage, while most people whose marriages go wrong are prepared to admit their mistakes and get out. In spite of the hand-wringing of politicians, bishops and leader writers, the only sense in which this is an obvious or urgent social problem is because of its impact on children: family break-up after divorce is seen as a relatively new phenomenon in contrast to the past when most children grew up in an intact family home with both parents present. Yet Lawrence Stone's research suggests a rather different interpretation of history, in which divorce has merely replaced death as the prime disrupting factor in marriages. There is no doubt, he writes, 'that lamentations over the collapse of the family in England are exaggerated, based on a failure to realize that in the past death was as important a cause of the premature dissolution of marriage as divorce is today'. In his book on marriage in England between 1500 and 1800, Stone describes the family in this period as 'a loose association of transients, constantly broken up by death of parents or children or the early departure of children from the home'.

According to this analysis, similar patterns of instability have always existed in family life. What is relatively new is the agent of disruption – unhappy spouses, a majority of them wives – and the financial burden marital breakdown places on the state. The political response, a rather feeble attempt to reinforce traditional marriage, ignores the explosive implication behind two hundred years of trends and statistics: that the institution was founded on an assumption of inequality between the sexes which fewer and fewer women are willing to accept. (They do not even, given the wide availability of effective contraception, need physical and financial protection during an adult life largely given over to child-bearing.) According to recent figures, almost a third of babies in Britain are now born outside wedlock, compared to only 13 per cent more than a decade ago. For these unmarried couples, it hardly matters whether MPs make divorce a bit harder, as they have already done, or propose something much more drastic. And politicians must be aware that any attempt severely to limit the grounds for divorce would simply put even more people off marriage, further accelerating its decline.

Their relative impotence is, in effect, a consequence of asking the wrong question. If marriage as a lifelong union no longer works for almost half the people who try it, it is time to ask whether we actually need state-sanctioned relationships – or, given the dramatic increase in life expectancy over previous centuries, whether it is reasonable to expect two people to live together until one of them dies. In that sense, getting married has come increasingly to resemble astrology, calling for predictions about future behaviour and events based on slender and deeply unscientific evidence. Fewer people are willing to take that chance, or to take it for the rest of their lives, but all governments and the Church have to offer is an anxious conviction that things are getting worse and a longing to turn the clock back fifty or even a hundred years. John Major tried it, in the shape of the short-lived back-to-basics campaign in the autumn and winter of 1993 whose emphasis on old-fashioned moral values was promptly undermined by the sexual unruliness of some of his own MPs (all of them, as it happens, men). What nostalgia has to offer, its sole antidote to the record rate of marital breakdown in Britain, is a return to the days when women surrendered their identities, their property, their incomes and their rights to their children – in effect their liberty – at the church or register office door. That is the brutal truth behind the British establishment's romantic vision of a golden age when men were men and women were Good Wives. Anyone for Victorian values?

The Last Silent Movie Star

THE FIRST ITEM to go under the hammer was a print of sea shells by a little-known artist, G. P. Trautner, with an estimated value of $700. The bidding shot up to $6,000, plus the auctioneer's premium of 15 per cent, causing intakes of breath and signalling the fierce contests that were to come. The second lot was another print by the same artist, which sold for $6,500, while some undistinguished Chinese porcelain dishes, worth no more than $100 each, made $6,900 a piece. A second-hand French textbook, decorated by its owner with doodles and dress designs, fetched $37,000. A tape-measure, silver-plated and valued at $500, realised an astonishing $48,875.

Even the sale catalogue, cover price $90 in hardback, sold nearly 90,000 copies – sufficient to rival a best-selling book. Fifteen thousand winners of a specially organised lottery were allowed to file past the furniture and personal possessions before the three-day sale began; two thousand people crowded into the saleroom, while 70,000 others faxed absentee bids on a special telephone line. The auction realised $4.5 million on the first night alone, producing headlines around the world announcing that it had already beaten all records. 'It's incredible,' Sotheby's president in New York, Diana Brooks, told reporters. 'It just shows you how people feel about their history.'

Yet these scenes of profligate expenditure reveal not so much what Americans feel about their past as their eagerness to participate in the rites of an extraordinary modern cult. The bidders who offered thousands of dollars for mundane domestic items belonging to a recently deceased woman were behaving no differently from those ardent Christians who scoured Europe in the Middle Ages in search of locks of hair, shards of bone and pieces of the True Cross. For centuries this brisk and lucrative trade was presided over uneasily by the Roman Catholic Church; in April 1996, the auction house Sotheby's assumed much the same role in orchestrating the disposal of the relics of Jackie Kennedy, who had died two years before from cancer. Just like the rusty nails, fragments of cloth and pieces of jewellery claimed by their vendors to have been touched by the Virgin Mary or St Catherine of Siena, the contents of the former First Lady's Fifth Avenue apartment were invested with a special value by association. Cures have not yet been claimed on their behalf, but the fake pearls Jackie wore in a famous photograph of herself and her young son in 1962 were one of the most sought-after items, recalling the miraculous healing gems supposedly found in the heart of a medieval saint, Margaret of Città di Castello, when her body was dissected after her death.

In the Middle Ages, female saints were more often associated with wonder-working relics than men, even though they made up fewer than a fifth of the saints' calendar; women, cynics might say, have always been expected to perform miracles. At least Jackie was spared the indignity of having her body parts fought over, unlike Mary Magdalen, whose arm was chewed by an over-enthusiastic thirteenth-century English bishop, Hugh of Lincoln, when he paid a visit to its supposed resting-place at Fécamp. The bishop, according to a modern commentator, 'defended himself to the horrified onlookers by replying that if he could touch the body of Christ in the mass, he could certainly apply his teeth to the Magdalen's bones'. The practice of investing body parts or possessions with special powers went on for centuries – essentially a belief in magic, which is why the Church felt so uncomfortable about it – and was satirised by the Italian writer Giuseppe Tomasi di Lampedusa in his epic novel *The Leopard*, about the decline of an aristocratic Sicilian family. The arbitrary, indeed random, aspect of the practice is exposed towards the end of the book when a papal inquiry team arrives to investigate the seventy-four supposed relics acquired over the years by the wealthy Salina sisters. The priest appointed to do the job is confronted by a motley collection of items, mounted in opulent frames and accompanied by illegible documents which allegedly verify their origins. Taking a practical approach, he sets about examining each bone or rag or tooth, prising the gilded frames apart and swiftly coming to a decision:

> Three hours later he re-emerged with his cassock full of dust and his hands black, but with a pleased look and a serene expression on his bespectacled face. He apologised for carrying a big wicker basket. 'I took the liberty of appropriating this to put in what I'd discarded; may I set it down here?' And he placed his burden in a corner; it was overflowing with torn papers and cards, little boxes containing bits of bone and gristle. 'I am happy to say that I have found five relics which are perfectly authentic and worthy of being objects of devotion. The rest are there,' he said, pointing at the basket. 'Could you tell me, Signorina, where I can brush myself down and wash my hands?'

How the priest has arrived at his decisions is never explained, which is the point of the scene; his judgement is no more scientific than that of the sisters, but it is backed by the weight of papal authority. Equally, the punters who shelled out an estimated $50 million on Jackie Kennedy's possessions could console themselves with the thought that the auction had been authorised – authenticated? – by her nearest relatives. They were, in that sense at least, getting value for their money. But what, in reality, were they spending it on? With its grossly inflated prices, the sale became a superstitious ritual, akin to buying into a legend; each dollar was a small but significant contribution to the process of confirming Jackie's place in that narrow firmament which was her destiny from the moment the assassin's shots rang out in Dallas in 1963. Narrow though not uncontested: Jackie has to share it with another of President Kennedy's women, the 'late' Marilyn Monroe, who sang a breathy 'happy birthday' to him at Madison Square Garden a few months before her own premature death in 1962. Marilyn and Jackie, mistress and wife, suicide blonde and grieving brunette: it was the brief Kennedy presidency which endowed the twentieth century with its most enduring female icons.

But what sort of women are they and why do they continue to have such power over us? Jacqueline Lee Bouvier, Jackie Kennedy, Jackie Onassis, Jackie O; it used to be a convention that women changed their names on marriage, but in this case it also means that she will forever be known – like Marilyn in a slightly different context – by the little-girl name that so neatly matches the little-girl voice. Childish in private, to all intents and purposes mute in public, Jackie's apotheosis came about through her extraordinary thirty-year silence after her husband's assassination. Her unusual reticence survived even the most lurid, not to say humiliating, revelations about Jack Kennedy's obsessive pursuit of extra-marital sex with secretaries, actresses and prostitutes, prompting Gore Vidal, her cousin-by-marriage, to characterise her as 'the last great silent movie star'. Marilyn Monroe achieved something similar by accident rather than design, securing unprecedented fame when she exited this world with a lethal cocktail of sleeping pills and alcohol. Each in her own way reinforces the iron rule that women, if they are to be truly admired, must be seen and not heard; indeed, the President's widow is a case study in how to win and keep public adoration, even managing to surmount the public relations disaster of her marriage to (and, at the time of his death in 1975, pending divorce from) the Greek shipping tycoon Aristotle Onassis. At her funeral in New York in April 1994, a 'private' event carried live by the big TV networks, one reporter announced that he would refer to her throughout as Mrs Kennedy, eerily underlining the way in which her rehabilitation had been completed by her death.

In the thirty years and six months between her husband's assassination and her own death, Jackie gave precisely two interviews. One was to the journalist Theodore White a week after Dallas, when she persuaded him to characterise the Kennedy presidency in an article for *Life* magazine as a version of Camelot: the mythical lost kingdom of King Arthur, made famous by the Lerner and Loewe musical whose soundtrack Jack Kennedy had frequently listened to on a record player at the White House. The effect of this behind-the-scenes intervention was far-reaching, as White admitted:

36

So the epitaph of the Kennedy administration became Camelot – a magic moment in American history when gallant men danced with beautiful women, when great deeds were done and when the White House became the center of the universe.

The other, to the author William Manchester, embroiled him and the Kennedy clan in endless trouble and recriminations when Jackie, having initially approached Manchester to write an official account of the assassination, took violent exception to the finished manuscript and threatened legal action to prevent publication. In the end, what she told Manchester on the record became the subject of an embargo, which means that almost no one reading these pages will be alive when it is finally released. At the time, Jackie's persecution of *The Death of a President* and its author drew critical comment but, in retrospect, it is clear that she knew what she was doing. For it was precisely this attribute – her self-imposed vow of silence – which was singled out for praise in a syrupy *Vanity Fair* profile rushed into print immediately after Jackie's death in 1994. 'In these days of public confession,' enthused the novelist and journalist Dominick Dunne, 'when we know far too much about far too many people, her silence became her strength and increased the admiration in which she was held.' Dunne recalled his one meeting with Jackie, at a publishing lunch in Manhattan, and the way she immediately put him at his ease: 'Only later did I realize that I had done all the talking. She had just given me the subject.'

Her death was a ticklish moment, for while Jackie herself might be (literally) as silent as the grave, others would not necessarily follow her example. The rule of *de mortuis nil nisi bonum* no longer exerts the force it once had and, if dirt was going to be dished, this was the time to expect it. *Vanity Fair* duly announced, in the summer of 1996, that it was going to run an extract from a book on the Kennedy marriage by one of its own writers, Edward Klein, prompting headlines which promised 'Book takes shine off Jackie O as paragon of virtue'. Yet the worst Klein's book could come up with was a claim that Jackie had lost her virginity to a previous boyfriend in a Paris lift; the *Vanity Fair* article turned out to have far more to say about the spectacular bad behaviour of the Kennedy *men*. Among its revelations was the claim that Jackie's father-in-law, the gruesome former ambassador Joe Kennedy, had forced her to listen to graphic and gynaecologically detailed accounts of his affairs with a variety of women; another was that, from the age of twenty-three, Jack Kennedy had suffered from a recurrent strain of gonorrhoea which was resistant to penicillin and other antibiotics. This did not prevent *Vanity Fair* billing Klein's book as the story of an arranged marriage, engineered for political motives, which became, 'against all odds . . . the start of a great love affair'. In effect, the extract marked a judicious rearranging of the furniture of the Camelot myth: the glamorous presidential couple, their image as doomed young lovers tarnished by sordid revelations about Jack Kennedy's womanising, were being subtly recast as players in a love story that triumphed over adversity. And much of that triumph was attributable, in this revised version, to the loyalty and courage of discreet, beautiful, suffering St Jackie.

She was, in a sense, born to the part. Three years younger than Marilyn Monroe, Jacqueline Lee Bouvier was born in 1929 and grew up in the 1940s, when adolescent girls were still being advised by their mothers to be good listeners and not let men know how clever they were. Her parents' marriage broke up because of 'Black Jack' Bouvier's gargantuan sexual appetite and legendary drinking, whereupon her mother remarried into the wealthy and socially well-connected Auchincloss family (Jackie's stepfather Hughdie had previously been married to Gore Vidal's mother, Nina Gore). The year she went to Vassar, a move that might have seemed overly studious in a girl whose career goal was so clearly marriage, Jackie made up for it by being chosen Debutante of the Year by social commentator Igor Cassini in his Cholly Knickerbocker column. He enthused:

> Queen Deb of the year is Jacqueline Bouvier, a regal brunette who has classic features and the daintiness of Dresden porcelain. She has poise, is soft-spoken and intelligent, everything the leading debutante should be. Her background is strictly 'Old Guard' . . .

So 'Old Guard' was Jackie that when she came first in a competition organised by *Vogue* magazine, her mother talked her out of accepting the prize, a trip to Paris, and promised to pay for her to spend the summer in Europe instead. On her return, an uncle pulled strings to get her a job variously described as 'Camera Girl' or 'Inquiring Photographer' for the *Washington Times-Herald*, where her interviewees included an old family friend, the journalist Arthur Krock; a Wall Street trader who briefly became her fiancé, John Husted; and the young Massachusetts senator Jack Kennedy. According to one biographical sketch of Jackie at this period, she sometimes shared her 'hatbox lunch' with Kennedy, her trip to France having 'taught her much about the pursuit of The Man'. But the relationship did not progress as smoothly as she would have liked. Kennedy took her to the Eisenhower inauguration, then failed to call for weeks. According to her stepsister Nina, she was 'besotted' with him and beside herself with anxiety; she turned for help to her mother, Janet, who provided a plan which might have come straight out of *The Rules*, the 1990s bestseller which advises women how to get a man. According to Ed Klein:

> Janet told Jackie where to shop for her clothes, how to do her hair, how often to see Jack, and what to say to him when he called. Janet even arranged for Jackie to go to England for the *Washington Times-Herald* to cover the forthcoming coronation of Queen Elizabeth.
>
> 'Should I see Jack before I leave?' Jackie asked.
>
> 'No,' said Janet. 'Tell him you're too busy and that you'll see him when you get back.'

This strategy worked, with a telegram from Kennedy arriving at the Mayfair flat where Jackie was staying, asking her to marry him. The wedding took place in September 1953, even though, again according to Klein, Kennedy confessed beforehand about his relentless promiscuity. 'She handled it pretty well,' said a family friend, Senator George Smathers, many years later. 'She was aware that Jack was a Kennedy, and that Joe had never been an example of virtue. Women of that class and generation were raised to turn a blind eye to sexual peccadilloes.' Perhaps Kennedy blamed his voracious sexual appetite on the medication he had to take for Addison's Disease, a progressive and life-threatening condition which destroys the immune system; the drugs, which included cortisone, are said to have increased his already abnormal libido. Whatever excuse he gave, his bride had some idea of what she was taking on when she walked down the aisle at St Mary's Church in Newport, Rhode Island, in a gown made of fifty yards of ivory taffeta faille with a tight-fitting bodice and bouffant skirt. Unsurprisingly, the marriage was rocky, with two separations and two reconciliations before Kennedy became his party's presidential candidate in September 1960.

At this point, though, politics began to take precedence over all other considerations. Martha Weinman, writing in the *New York Times*, captured the mood of the moment – and Jackie's importance in feminising her husband's campaign – in a despatch which read:

> When Jacqueline Kennedy, then five days the wife of the Presidential candidate, stepped aboard the family yacht in Hyannis Port, wearing an orange pullover sweater, shocking pink Capri pants and a bouffant hairdo that gamboled merrily in the breeze, even those newsmen present who could not tell shocking pink from Windsor rose, knew they were witnessing something of possible political consequences.

Benefiting from comparisons with her predecessor, the much older Mamie Eisenhower, Jackie's image was new and striking. Yet her role as First Lady was traditional, whether she was acting as hostess at glamorous parties for visiting heads of state or renovating the White House; there was already a sense that she represented what Betty Friedan, only two years later, would denounce in *The Feminine Mystique*. During her short reign as First Lady, Jackie was viewed either as a classy clothes horse who inspired endless articles about her favourite designers – a staggering amount of information is available on the clothes she wore at each and every official function – or as a spendthrift who wasted money on her wardrobe and costly alterations to the presidential apartments. Her entertaining was on such a lavish scale that it quickly attracted criticism, her party at Mount Vernon for President Ayub Khan of Pakistan being a notable example. Wearing white lace with a chartreuse sash, Jackie had her guests transported by boat from Washington to the site of the party, prompting the *New York Herald-Tribune* to comment:

> Among the items paid for by the government, so far as could be learned, were the cost of hauling three generators to Mount Vernon to operate the special electric wiring installed in the mansion for the party; the cost of operating the four boats that took the guests to the party and back; the fuel for a fleet of Marine Corps buses that transported twenty-two White House butlers and Marine Corps and Navy personnel to the party, and gasoline for the White House limousines that brought guests from the dock to the mansion.

Jackie's innovations, as First Lady, involved trivial adjustments such as abolishing receiving lines at official parties. Yet on the day of the assassination, 22 November 1963, all this was forgotten; Jackie's transformation to symbol of a nation was virtually instantaneous. In those stunned moments after her husband's death, she was omnipresent: standing beside Lyndon Johnson on Air Force One as he was sworn in as President, still in her blood-spattered suit; paying a dramatic small-hours visit to her husband's body as it lay in state in the Great Rotunda of the Capitol; kneeling with her small daughter Caroline to kiss the hem of the American flag draping his coffin.

Omnipresent and omni-silent. Everyone else had their say, world leaders and ordinary people, talking freely about the loss they felt and the political impact of Kennedy's death. Jackie said almost *nothing*. Her picture was flashed round the world, appearing in newspapers and on TV; *The Times*, whose unnamed correspondents were visibly moved by her presence, quoted her only once in all its coverage of the assassination and its aftermath – and then indirectly. 'The President was wounded in the head,' the paper reported on Saturday 23 November 1963, 'and collapsed into the arms of his wife. She was heard to cry, "Oh no" as she cradled his head in her lap and the car, spattered with blood, speeded to Parkland Hospital.'

Oh no: these two words, shocked and disbelieving, were Jackie Kennedy's reaction to an event which wrecked her life and, arguably, changed world history. Later, as Air Force One aproached Andrews Air Force Base near Washington, she refused to change her blood-stained clothes. 'Let them see what they've done,' she said. 'I want them to see.' Already Jackie was making herself a symbol, a point which was not lost on *The Times*. 'The drama took full and appalling effect the moment [Mrs Kennedy] stepped from the aircraft,' said its report of the plane's arrival. Her 'frail figure' dominated the paper's coverage over the next few days.

At one level, Jackie's grief acted as a focus and a release; her dignity set an example at a time when many people were too shocked to know how to behave. Yet her bereavement also moved her into a different league of stardom. Andy Warhol, whose instinct for fame was ruthless and infallible, did not produce a single image of Jackie until she was widowed, whereupon she became something of an obsession. A year after the assassination he created *Red Jackie*, a cruel mockery of 1960s femininity which superimposes garish poster colours on Jackie's rather delicate facial features. The picture's title, and its background of unrelenting red, serve as insistent reminders of the moment when she was showered with her husband's blood. In the same year Warhol produced the *Jackie Triptych*, three photographic images of Jackie at the funeral which consciously played on religious iconography – she was, like her husband, a Roman Catholic – to turn her into a *mater dolorosa*. Two years later he created *Jackie III*, a four-frame silk screen in which the happy young wife is cruelly transformed into a grieving widow. Warhol was equally fascinated by Marilyn Monroe, but not until after her death in 1962, when he promptly created *The Two Marilyns* – a diptych in black-and-white and blaring colours which looks forward to *Red Jackie* two years later. This was the first of dozens of images Warhol created of the star, becoming ever more abstract and reified in the period leading up to his own death in 1987.

The cover of *Goddess*, Anthony Summers's warts-and-all biography of Marilyn, showed her wiping away a tear, capitalising on his readers' prurient curiosity about her unhappiness. The last shreds of the actress's dignity were dramatically swept away when a photograph of her corpse – taken, ghoulishly, after the physical intrusion of the post-mortem had been carried out – was published both in Summers's book and in a British Sunday newspaper. Yet the more we know about Marilyn's misery – her abortions, her addiction to sleeping pills, her doomed love affairs with Jack and Bobby Kennedy – the more popular she becomes. Hillary Clinton was viewed with unprecedented sympathy when she went on TV, during her husband's first presidential campaign and in the wake of revelations about his affair with Gennifer Flowers, and stood by her man. Even Margaret Thatcher prompted an uncharacteristic wave of public sympathy during her premiership when her son Mark briefly got lost in a desert and she wept in public. Like Warhol's exploitation of Marilyn and Jackie, so nakedly rooted in their personal tragedies, these examples combine to tell a harsh truth about our fascination with famous women: we like our icons best when they are in distress.

A decade after the Kennedy assassination, Warhol knew Jackie well enough to escort her and her sister Lee Radziwill to an exhibition of Egyptian art at the Brooklyn Museum. During the journey to the museum, Jackie quizzed him about another star whose portrait he had turned into a silk screen, and with whom he had recently appeared in a film, Elizabeth Taylor. It was Jackie's extraordinary fame, however, that interested Warhol:

> We finally reached the museum. As we wandered through the galleries, every person there seemed to recognise Jackie. They whispered among themselves. You could hear her name in the air: 'Jackie . . . Jackie . . . Jackie.' It was weird.

It shouldn't have been weird at all, especially for Warhol, who had played a significant role in elevating Jackie beyond the realm of ordinary stardom in the first place. Silence and grief are a potent combination, as he well knew, disabling the darker emotions which wealthy and seemingly powerful women might otherwise stir up – envy, fear, anger. In one sense, Jackie's public image could have been created with this purpose in mind, long before the assassination: it consisted of beauty but not too much in the way of brains, glamour but no real power, and a veneer of modernity which barely concealed a commitment to a type of femininity which was already becoming outmoded when she became First Lady in 1961 (an old friend once described it, although Jackie grew up in New England, as 'a Southern routine . . . being both dumb and attractive to men'). The success of her role in what she retrospectively christened Camelot depended on these elements, although in other respects the analogy does not stand up to more than a moment's inspection. The love triangle which poisoned King Arthur's mythical court was King/Queen/*Queen's* lover (Arthur/Guinevere/Lancelot) not President/First Lady/President's Mistress (Jack/Jackie/Marilyn); Jackie's reordering of history, only a week after the assassination, shows that she was already creating a protective myth for her dead husband. Jack Kennedy was now the murdered king, betrayed by an assassin's bullets, rather than the man who had betrayed *her* time and time again with other women. In those more innocent days, when Jackie talked about Camelot to Theodore White for his article in *Life* magazine, there was every reason to think that the secret of Jack's multiple infidelities was safe; although his predatory sexual habits were known to, even notorious among, Secret Service agents, the FBI and some well-informed journalists, a convention that the President's private life was off-limits was still universally respected.

A more interesting question is the nature of the betrayal of which Jackie, in her Guinevere role, was tacitly accusing herself. There is little evidence, apart from a rumoured affair with the actor William Holden, that she was unfaithful to Jack Kennedy; while many observers have mentioned her beauty, almost no one seems to have considered her sexy. The most likely answer is her split-second reaction after the shots were fired in Dallas, captured by Abraham Zapruder's home movie footage, when she began scrambling out of the open-topped limousine in an attempt to save herself. Unlike Nellie Connally, who shielded her wounded husband with her own body, and in contradistinction to the *Times* report, the film shows Jackie inadvertently kicking the President's head as she crawled on to the boot, aiming for a rubber handhold at the rear until a Secret

Service agent, Clint Hill, pushed her back inside the car. Jackie told the Warren Commission, which investigated the assassination, that she had no recollection of trying to escape, an understandable lapse of memory which may have made the evidence of the Zapruder film even harder to live with. 'Her momentary loss of courage was not featured by the media,' wrote Jackie's biographer David Heymann, although it soon became public knowledge when the Zapruder footage was shown over and over again on television. But when Dominick Dunne observed many years later in *Vanity Fair* that on the day of the assassination 'her image became engraved on our souls', it was not those seconds of paralysis and fugue he had in mind but her grief-stricken composure in the hours and days afterwards. (How potent this image was can be gauged by the recollection of another American journalist, too young to remember the actual shooting, of how she borrowed one of her mother's hats – it had a small veil, like the one she had seen Jackie wear in press cuttings – and walked slowly to school pretending to be the President's widow in her husband's funeral procession.)

Her initial panic does mean, however, that the myth of St Jackie almost failed to get off the ground at the very moment of her martyrdom. This is not a criticism of her instinctive human reaction to save herself under gunfire, nor does it indicate a moral weakness as profound as Jack Kennedy's in cynically parading his family and indulging in public displays of uxoriousness during his presidency. But the fact that Jackie's image was not tarnished by the Zapruder film is a testament to how badly she was needed, as a focus, in the aftermath of the assassination. What *is* surprising is that her role as Camelot's tragic queen has been able to withstand, over three decades, any number of revelations about the real nature of the Kennedy presidency. Indeed, her stock has continued to rise as that of the Kennedy clan has fallen, as though the naming of Jack's mistresses or exposure of his father's sexual braggadocio merely serve to cast her in an ever more beatific light. (Relentless reporting of Marilyn Monroe's promiscuity and emotional collapses have peformed a parallel function, characterising her as the blonde airhead to Jackie's dark Madonna.) When Jackie died, her role as a secular American saint was dramatically confirmed by the thou- sands of relic-hunters who were prepared to make so substantial an investment – financial and emotional – in mundane objects she had touched or which had once stood in her apartment.

One practical result of Jackie's canonisation is that she continues to cast a long shadow over more recent First Ladies and women who aspire, however slim their chances of achieving it, to that position. Hillary Clinton, young enough to be judged by her appearance even though the role of clothes horse does not come naturally to her, underwent rapid and bewildering changes of image in the early months of the first Clinton presidency, suggesting she was sensitive on the subject without knowing quite how to get it right. Although she could never be Jackie – and it seems unlikely that that has ever been one of her ambitions – her decision to secure political power through her marriage inevitably invited comparisons with her glamorous predecessor. (The situation was not helped by the way in which her husband's administration initially cultivated resemblances with Camelot, intentionally casting Bill Clinton in Jack Kennedy's image. For if Bill was Jack's heir, where did that leave Hillary?) The lesson she and her husband's advisers learned, slowly and painfully, is that an icon is a two-dimensional image, resonant in its visual impact but static and unable to answer back; formidably articulate and entrusted with the job of radically overhauling the country's health care programme, Hillary was too substantial a person to fit within this narrow frame and duly suffered for it. Her retreat from the much-vaunted Clinton co-presidency into the role of supportive wife and concerned mother was humiliating and not wholly convincing, even as she threw herself into producing a mawkish book about raising children, *It Takes a Village*. At the Democratic convention in Chicago in August 1996, Hillary took a leaf out of Elizabeth Dole's book in allowing herself to be photographed throwing admiring glances at her husband; Mrs Dole, a former transportation secretary in President Reagan's cabinet, had nimbly repackaged herself as Political Wife days before when, apparently without embarrassment, she got up and told delegates at the Republican convention, which confirmed her husband as presidential candidate, Why She Loved Her Man. The filmed biography which preceded Bill Clinton's convention speech included, according to the *Guardian*, 'shots of Mr Clinton in the

Oval Office, playing with his baby nephew, and – rewriting the story of a famously strained marriage – endless stills of embraces and lingering looks between Mr Clinton and his wife Hillary'. (In Britain, Cherie Booth, the lawyer-wife of Tony Blair, went in for similar displays of public devotion in the months after her husband was elected leader of the Labour Party.)

With the presidential election looming in November that year, Hillary Clinton and Elizabeth Dole were, for the moment at least, safely back in the closet. Yet the problem will not go away. From the Virgin Mary to Marilyn Monroe, our icons are women we admire because they have made a sacrifice – in blood or ambition and preferably in both. James McGuigan, a Clinton supporter who enthused after the 1996 Chicago convention that 'Bill Clinton is my generation's JFK', was expressing more than the nostalgia of the thirty-something Democrat for a prelapsarian dream he is too young to remember; his observation was also a warning about the role intelligent, forceful women are still expected to play. If Hillary Clinton wants to inspire even a fraction of the admiration showered on Jackie Kennedy over the last three decades, she needs more than a new hairstyle or dress designer. What she needs is a tragedy.

Our Lady of the Test Tubes

IT'S NOT MUCH of a part, really – very few lines and nothing at all in the way of stage directions. A mild expression of surprise is allowed, gratitude certainly, but she isn't expected to display unseemly emotion. It's true that the news is unexpected, and awkwardly timed in view of her recent engagement, but she has a few months to get used to it (what's happened may be a bit of a departure from the normal procedure, but not by *that* much). Everyone knows that congratulations are in order on these occasions, and the only effective difference between this and any other pregnancy is that she is getting that extra bit of notice, and the way in which the conventional roles are reversed; women usually get to tell their partners, not the other way round, and it's rare to use an intermediary. Especially one who's a total stranger to at least one of the parties, but we'll overlook that little piece of thoughtlessness in view of the unique circumstances of the case. Let's concentrate instead on the tranquillity of the scene, its essential benevolence, and the signs and gestures which express the new mother-to-be's humble acceptance of her condition. The Renaissance artist Fra Filippo Lippi, in a classic fifteenth-century version of the scene, painted her on a low seat, eyes downcast, a missal in one hand and the other already protectively cradling her belly. The angel watches from a respectful distance, as though he is simultaneously relieved by the smooth reception of his announcement – you never can tell with women – and very slightly curious about her failure to protest. There are no awkward statistics here, no mention of the extremely low success rate – 7.9 per cent – of artificial insemination as a method of conception, just an awareness that they have each fulfilled their allotted roles and a suggestion, no more than a hint perhaps but it's inherent in the composition, that her quiet acquiescence might even lead to a restoration of the prelapsarian state of grace lost through the disobedience and inquisitiveness of her ancestor, Eve. For if she were to lift her head for a moment, looking out from the sumptuous loggia in which she is seated, she would see a path bordered by flowering plants and beckoning her into a delightful garden; it does not require much imagination, especially with the divine figure of the angel in its midst, to interpret this pastoral scene as the silent promise, as a reward for her exemplary behaviour, of a return to Eden.

The neo-classicist Nicolas Poussin, a couple of hundred years later, dispensed with most of Lippi's props and concentrated on the relationship between the two protagonists, supplying them with flushed cheeks and, on her side, the closed eyes and uplifted face of someone experiencing near-orgasmic rapture. The angel's hands gesture bossily, like a demented traffic policeman, giving the impression that the procedure's got a bit more complicated in the intervening period and needs careful supervision if it is to succeed. Follow my instructions closely, he seems to be saying, and her out-stretched palms imply ecstatic submission to this firm advice. More to the point, her posture – she is seated on a sort of low platform, arms thrown back and knees raised, Bible at her feet – eerily creates an empty space in the centre of her body which will, very soon, be filled with the foetus whose arrival the angel has just announced.

Let's fast-forward to the 1990s and the scene has changed again. On our left is Mandy Allwood, would-be mother of octuplets, flanked by her PR consultant, Max Clifford. On our right, in place of the angel, is the first in a series of doctors, the Midlands GP who prescribed the fertility drugs that brought about Allwood's unprecedented multiple pregnancy. Behind him, in the space which used to be occupied by a benign but invisible deity, are all the other men in the case: the newspaper editor who furiously denies offering a cash sum per surviving baby for her story, the anti-abortion campaigner who insists that there should be no intervention in the pregnancy, and last but not least Paul Hudson, the proud father, unable to disguise his satisfaction at what he appears to take as a tribute to his sexual prowess. 'I'm ecstatic,' Mandy announces, but her story ends in a matter of weeks, not months, and the image that remains indelibly associated with her is not the longed-for realisation of a modern Madonna and child(ren) but a harrowing series of miscarriages and eight tiny coffins. Soon, though, Mandy is hosting her own phone-in show on a national radio station – the modern equivalent, perhaps, of a travelling freak show – in dubious compensation for the loss not only of her unborn babies but of the son she already had, whose father successfully applied for custody after his erstwhile partner's abrupt elevation to national celebrity. This, then, is the irony of Mandy Allwood's modern morality tale: her determination to give birth to a record number of babies ends in a kind of barrenness worse than that which drove her to ask her GP for fertility treatment in the first place. Her painful, public trajectory – from mother-of-one to mother-of-none in record time – is an extraordinarily high price to pay for attempting to live out a fantasy. (In 1997, it was announced that she was pregnant again, this time with one foetus.)

Yet so seductive was Allwood's vision of multiple motherhood that many people, most of them not directly involved and including a variety of personages who should have known better, rushed to reinforce it. The egregious Professor Jack Scarisbrick, chairman of the anti-abortion organisation *Life*, demanded that Allwood be kept 'out of the hands of the killers' – his term for the consultants who argued that selective abortion was the only way of sustaining the pregnancy – and mused that one day 'people will see the row of children alongside her in bed and will say "how lovely". I hope they will also remember the doom-and-gloom talk from the doctors'. Yet the outcome, unless Allwood allowed the doctors to intervene again and destroy some of the embryos, was never in doubt. The human female was not designed for multiple births on this scale and 'allowing nature to take its course', as advocated by some of the participants in the noisy public debate which followed the sale of her story to the *News of the World*, always meant the death of some and probably all of the foetuses, as well as a considerable risk to Allwood herself. Just how perilous her actual physical condition was, in contradistinction to the insouciant pronouncements in newspapers along the lines of 'the more, the merrier', became clear as she began to miscarry in the nineteenth week of the pregnancy, initially losing three of her octuplets. The *Evening Standard* reported that 'Mandy needs a miracle now' and the doctor in charge of her case confirmed that her uterus was still 'very, very overstretched', comparing it to an overinflated balloon. Later the same week, she lost all five remaining foetuses. This was undoubtedly a personal tragedy, although some commentators questioned the ease with which she had been prescribed drugs to stimulate her ovaries when she and Hudson, who both had children by previous partners, were not obvious candidates for fertility treatment (she had also, it emerged, ignored her GP's advice that she and Hudson should abstain from sex immediately after starting the treatment). What wasn't questioned was where Allwood acquired her transparently unrealistic view of pregnancy and why she clung to it so stubbornly, even to the point of losing all her potential babies. Faced with what was literally a life-or-death choice, Allwood simply arranged herself for newspaper photographs in poses of Madonna-like serenity, smiling and cradling her belly as though she had not the slightest inkling of impending disaster. Like one of those female saints stoically contemplating martyrdom in a Renaissance predella, she radiated a sense of being protected by a higher force. *Amor vincit omnia*; mother love, she seemed to be saying, conquers all.

In the West, our pattern for maternal behaviour was for centuries the Blessed Virgin Mary, whose career, from the Annunciation to her appearance as a radiant young mother, provided the only approved images not just of maternity but of womanhood itself. Her redemptive function, hinted at in Renaissance art, was made explicit by Pope Paul VI in the *Credo of the People of God* when he hailed the Virgin as 'the new Eve': by patiently accepting her lot, Mary made up for the sin of her ancestor, the all-singing, all-dancing bad girl of Christian cosmography. When women went to church, when they studied the Bible or listened to it being read aloud if they were illiterate, in the pictures they saw in public places and at home, the message they got was one and the same: this was the model they should strive to emulate. In wealthy households, even domestic objects reminded them of their obligations; the

Filippo Lippi Annunciation mentioned above, for instance, was originally painted on one of the panels of a *cassone*, the type of large wooden chest which was a standard item of furniture in homes in the Early Modern period. Many women must have known the passage in Luke's Gospel describing the Annunciation, our fullest source for the story of Jesus's conception, more or less by heart:

> And the angel came in unto her, and said, Hail, thou that art highly favoured, the Lord is with thee: blessed art thou among women.
>
> And when she saw him, she was troubled at his saying, and cast in her mind what manner of salutation this should be.
>
> And the angel said unto her, Fear not, Mary: for thou hast found favour with God.
>
> And, behold, thou shalt conceive in thy womb, and bring forth a son, and shalt call his name JESUS.
>
> He shall be great, and shall be called the Son of the Highest: and the Lord God shall give unto him the throne of his father David:
>
> And he shall reign over the house of Jacob for ever; and of his kingdom there shall be no end.
>
> Then said Mary unto the angel, How shall this be, seeing I know not a man?
>
> And the angel answered and said unto her, The Holy Ghost shall come upon thee, and the power of the Highest shall overshadow thee: therefore also that holy thing which shall be born of thee shall be called the Son of God.
>
> And, behold, thy cousin Elisabeth, she hath also conceived a son in her old age: and this is the sixth month with her, who was called barren.
>
> For with God nothing shall be impossible.
>
> And Mary said, Behold the handmaid of the Lord; be it unto me according to thy word. And the angel departed from her.

Ecce ancilla domini: the status of the Virgin in this iconic scene is no better than that of a servant in the household of a higher

53

male authority. It is not a huge leap from the notion that women's bodies are at men's disposal in this way to the assumption that it is *all* they are – receptacles or vessels, without individual will, ready for use. This striking example of synecdoche, in which one part of the body, the uterus, comes to stand for the whole, soon became institutionalised within the Roman Catholic Church. The litany of Loreto, for example, a prayer in use since the thirteenth century, eulogises the Virgin in a series of images which are both inanimate and remarkable for their association with hollow objects or buildings: she is the Spiritual Vase, the Vase of Honour, the Vase of Remarkable Devotion, the House of God, the Tower of David, the Tower of Ivory, the House of Gold and the Ark of the Covenant. Vases are containers, just waiting to be filled up; houses and towers are spaces for someone to inhabit; the ark is a chest or box: all are metaphors for the womb. The association of women and hollowness is pervasive; even today, in secular culture, women are stigmatised as 'bags' or, even worse, '*old* bags' – the adjective adding the sense of 'worn out' or 'overused' to the initial image of emptiness. The word 'bag' is, according to Jane Mills's book *Womanwords*, one of several in the English language which 'suggest a woman is an empty container or vessel, one presumed available to be "filled up" by a man'. Indeed, the phrase 'the weaker vessel', instantly recognisable as a synonym for 'woman', has been in almost permanent use since 1526, when William Tyndale employed it in his English translation of the New Testament. According to the historian Anthony Fletcher, in his authoritative analysis of gender in the Early Modern period:

> 'A woman is the weaker vessel' quickly became an established proverb: it runs through the conduct book literature of the pre-civil war period and recurs in sermons. Preaching at St Paul's Cross in 1601, for example, John Dove discussed why husbands should respect their 'weaker vessel' wives, citing Ephesians, chapter 5. The proverb is also common in Shakespeare. The country girl Jaquenetta, caught with Costard in the King's park at the opening of *Love's Labour's Lost*, is characterised by Don Adriano as 'the weaker vessel which I apprehended with the aforesaid swain' ... The

notion here of relative emptiness carries all the resonances of the gender order upon which scriptural patriarchy rested, resonances of man's strength, initiative and authority.

Fletcher's emphasis here is on what the phrase 'the weaker vessel' implied, by contrast, about men. But the speed with which it spread through popular and high culture, and its enduring popularity, suggests that it embodied a theory about women which was promptly understood and widely appreciated. This is because it reflected not just the Christian view of women as receptacles but a parallel medical tradition stretching back to the second century AD and the Greek doctor Galen, personal physician to the Roman emperor Marcus Aurelius and the author of influential surviving texts on anatomy. Galen carried out his investigations into the structure of the body during the Roman Empire, but his work in its turn drew on a much more ancient tradition, summarising much of the medical knowledge – or what was for centuries accepted as knowledge – of the ancient world. His followers regarded the uterus as a troubling (and occasionally wandering) void which, in Fletcher's modern formulation, 'needed to be fortified by being put to the use for which it was intended; women were seen, paradoxically in view of the hazards and pains involved, as becoming healthier by regular pregnancies'. This was also the view of the fifth-century BC philosopher Plato, who confidently announced that the womb 'longs to generate children. When it remains barren too long after puberty, it is distressed and sorely disturbed and straying about the body and cutting off passages of the breath, it impedes respiration and provokes all manner of diseases besides'. (Unsurprisingly, perhaps, in view of the weight of this body of opinion, the Greek word for womb – *hustera* – is the root of the word 'hysteria'.) Yet even in Plato's time, the association of women and receptacles was already long-established; the Greek poet Hesiod, who lived around 700 BC, included the story of Pandora's box in his *Works and Days*, describing how a woman's curiosity about the *pithos* or storage jar entrusted to her led to the unleashing of untold evils on the world. In this alternative version of the Adam and Eve myth, Pandora is not a 'spiritual vase' like the Virgin but a troublesome meddler whose box, far from being empty, contains a multitude of unpleasant things. There is an echo here of another belief popular with medical authorities until as late as the eighteenth century, which was that the womb, if it was not kept clean by regular pregnancies, had a tendency to fill up with unpleasant substances: 'So artificially indeed is a woman formed,' according to a treatise on women's ailments written by John Ball in 1770, 'that at some stated seasons that redundancy of blood may be discharged.' In other words women's bodies, when not fulfilling the purpose for which they were created, were defective and problematic. Anthony Fletcher again:

> Imprisoned by a gender stereotype which was founded on the Old Testament and ancient Greek medical texts, [English doctors] were unable to break free from a notion of women's inferiority and weakness which constrained any positive advance in real understanding of women's bodies.

But the consequences were even more far-reaching than that. For centuries, biblical ideas about a woman's proper and indeed only role, and medical notions about the defective construction of the female body, combined to create a model in which members of the female sex were seen as worryingly, dangerously hollow until they were 'filled up' by pregnancy. As it happened, all but the wealthiest and most educated had little choice in the matter; the absence of reliable methods of contraception, especially after the early church fathers set out deliberately to destroy a corpus of knowledge on the subject from the ancient world, meant that the vast majority of women fulfilled their destiny not once but many times over. Quite often they died as a result of it, but neither the Roman Catholic nor the Protestant churches saw this as a problem. Martin Luther, the Augustinian monk who launched the Reformation in 1517, was merely expressing a widely held conviction when he observed: 'If women get tired and die of bearing, there is no harm in that; let them die as long as they bear; they were made for that.' For most of recorded history, such a view would not even have been controversial.

What has all this to do with Mandy Allwood? By the time she

embarked on her ill-fated attempt to become pregnant in the spring of 1996, things had changed dramatically. Allwood had not been 'chosen' but had brought about her predicament herself, with help from her boyfriend and the fertility drugs prescribed by her GP. Yet her blind acceptance of the unsustainable pregnancy she had created, and her refusal to take an active role in trying to avert the inevitable consequence, make sense only in a climate in which motherhood has acquired more mystique than ever – so much so, in fact, that nothing, not even the prospect of foetal or maternal death, is allowed to interfere with a woman's determination to achieve it. This, as it happens, is exactly the message which has been promulgated in recent years in countries where sophisticated medical techniques permit and even encourage women to conceive and carry babies to term in circumstances which would previously have ruled out one or both processes. It's ironic that, at the very moment in history when women finally have a choice of when and indeed whether to have children, our most urgent obsession is not how to use this new-found freedom but how to ensure that more women, not fewer, have babies. The emphasis is now firmly on *in*fertility: scare stories about a decline in sperm counts proliferate, while newspapers and magazines are full of features about women struggling to become pregnant in the face of every imaginable obstacle. Women routinely embark on treatments which enable them to get pregnant regardless of their age, state of health or level of fertility: in 1993, a 58-year-old London woman conceived twins after treatment by the controversial Italian gynaecologist Professor Severino Antinori, who believes that having babies is 'an inalienable civil right'; in 1996, the *Mail on Sunday* bought the story of a woman who had acted as a surrogate mother on behalf of her grown-up daughter, who had fertile eggs but was born without a womb, and her son-in-law.

Very little consideration has been given, thus far, to the question of the impact on children of having parents old enough to be their grandparents, or the confusion in surrogacy cases about who is the 'real' mother; the fact that men are able to conceive children into their eighties, the argument most frequently deployed in support of post-menopausal mothers, ignores the reality that few people would choose to have parents two or three generations older than themselves (and, therefore, likely to die while they are in infancy). But we should not be surprised that women go to such lengths to have children, given the horror that now attaches to a diagnosis of infertility and the insistence of doctors working in the field that everything can and must be done to correct it. Professor Ian Craft, one of the most high-profile practitioners in Britain of IVF (*in vitro* fertilisation, where eggs are removed from a woman's ovaries, fertilised with donor sperm in a laboratory, and the resulting embryos implanted in her womb), believes that for most people, discovering they are infertile is harder to deal with than being told they have cancer. 'There is', he says, 'an enormous burden of continuing grief.' Other doctors have gone further, suggesting that becoming pregnant is so vital to a woman's mental health that helping the infertile should take precedence over treatment for life-threatening diseases. These are not, it should be emphasised, rogue views within the medical profession; in 1993, Professor Richard Lilford, head of obstetrics and gynaecology at Leeds General Infirmary, actually argued that infertility treatment 'should come before chemotherapy for advanced cancers, before hip replacements and before cataract surgery'.

This staggering reversal – giving priority to elective medical procedures over treatment which saves lives, restores mobility and repairs sight – is a graphic demonstration of the extraordinary value which currently attaches to conception. Yet the techniques in question are not just expensive – another high-profile practitioner of IVF, Professor (now Lord) Robert Winston, put the cost of that procedure somewhere between £1,400 and £2,200 in a recent book – but have a dauntingly high failure rate. A study published in the *Lancet* in November 1996 reported that women of twenty-five to thirty stand a 16 per cent chance of getting pregnant through IVF, while the success rate falls to 7 per cent – one in fourteen – for a forty-year-old. Infertility treatment is invasive and raises hopes which will almost certainly be dashed; in their book *Pandora's Clock: Understanding Our Fertility*, which is broadly sympathetic to women who choose to undergo fertility treatment, Maureen Freely and Celia Pyper observe that 'even those patients who receive the most considerate treatment show signs of emotional scarring'. One woman who tried IVF without becoming pregnant told Freely and Pyper: 'I know they meant well, but they treated my body as if it were a box of cornflakes.'

However well-intentioned doctors are, the consequences of unsuccessful treatment are not difficult to imagine. Told she has a condition worse than cancer; invited to contemplate treatments costing thousands of pounds, possibly of her own money; facing techniques which would have belonged, as little as three decades ago, in the realms of science fiction; when IVF fails, a woman's initial sense of inadequacy is horribly reinforced. At the same time, the expenditure of so much time, money and effort underlines the idea that pregnancy is the *sine qua non*, the defining moment, of a woman's life. With this as the prevailing ideology, it should come as no surprise to discover that, in a bizarre handful of recent cases, women have had babies while in a coma and unaware of the process, or even of the fact they were pregnant. Here are some of those cases:

- July 1993, California. A brain-dead woman, shot in the head four months before while attempting unsuccessfully to burgle a house, gives birth to a boy in an Oakland hospital. Her life support machine is then turned off.

- December 1995, Hampshire. Sarah Mapes, twenty-two collapses with a brain haemorrhage and slips into a coma. She is twenty weeks pregnant, and doctors consult her boyfriend, Steven Davies, and her parents about whether to keep her body functioning until the baby can be delivered. Her parents insist that the pregnancy must continue and, as next-of-kin, their wishes take precedence over Davies's stated preference that she be allowed to die. Five months later, without recovering consciousness, Mapes gives birth to a son.

- New Year's Eve, 1995, New York. Doctors break the news to the parents of a young woman, lying in a hospital bed in a persistent vegetative state since a car crash,

59

that their daughter is five months pregnant. The pregnancy is the result of a rape which has taken place in the hospital while the patient was deeply unconscious and unable to defend herself. The parents decide that the pregnancy should go ahead, and in March 1996 their daughter gives birth to a son at the Strong Memorial Hospital in Rochester.

In the last of these three cases, the grandparents were explicit about why they wanted their daughter to give birth to the unknown rapist's child: even if she failed to recover, they reasoned, they would at least keep 'some part of her'. What the young woman would have thought, on waking and discovering she had become a mother in these grim circumstances, is a question they do not seem to have addressed; the possibility that she was aware of what was happening throughout, as in the case of a small number of patients who have recovered from a supposed vegetative state, is simply too dreadful to contemplate. Decisions of this sort, now being taken more frequently thanks to improved technology, have given rise to the cruel but accurate phrase 'souvenir babies' to describe births deliberately engineered by doctors after the mothers' effective demise. (A childless British widow, Diane Blood, made headlines in autumn 1996 for her attempt to apply the same logic to men; she wished to use sperm taken from her husband's unconscious body, as he lay dying of meningitis, to impregnate herself. Blood's crusade, and her court battle to gain access to the sperm gathered by a process known as electro-ejaculation, have engendered many column inches of sympathetic coverage, even from commentators not usually known for their compassionate views on women who voluntarily become single mothers.) What these cases have in common, and where they have parallels with Mandy Allwood's drug-induced multiple pregnancy, is the idea that women are somehow 'empty' or incomplete if they do not have children, or as many children as they would like, and that this justifies medical intervention on almost any scale. Few people – Allwood and her doctors, the attendants of the brain-dead women described above – are confronted with the unpleasant practical results of applying this principle. But Steven Davies has described what happened to his unconscious girlfriend, Sarah Mapes, as her pregnancy progressed:

> It seems so simple – a baby to replace the life that has gone. But on the inside it's a horror movie. Sarah swelled from seven to fifteen stone because of the steroids, her eyeballs were taped into the sockets; her hair was matted. She had no dignity left. I asked the doctors, 'why are you doing this?' and they replied, 'because we can'. What's the difference between a doctor and God? Jack isn't a miracle baby. He is a manufactured baby. Will we get to the point where a couple have a crash and if the woman dies the doctors will ask the husband if they had sex the night before because she may have conceived and they might be able to keep the pregnancy going?

Cases likes this one make a mockery of the notion of informed consent, the ground on which the Human Fertilisation and Embryology Authority initially turned down Diane Blood's request to use her dead husband's sperm. (She was eventually allowed, after a court hearing, to take his sperm abroad for treatment in a fertility clinic.) Steven Davies raised the issue with his girlfriend's doctors but they were unimpressed: 'I tried to argue with the doctors that she wouldn't have wanted it, but they said, "she's a woman. She would have wanted the baby to live". When I said, "not all women are the same", they refused to listen.'

The doctors' assumption in this case that they knew best is typical of experts in almost any field, but their justification for allowing the pregnancy to continue – that every woman would want to have a child, regardless of her circumstances – is a cultural rather than a medical decision. Although it is unlikely that they gave the matter any thought, their behaviour is exactly like that of the angel in Luke's Gospel, whose announcement to the Virgin of her impending pregnancy brooks no argument. Indeed, the old biblical injunction – go forth and multiply – has, thanks to advances in medicine, taken on a sinister new resonance. Our grandmothers might envy the contraceptive techniques which have, for the first time in history, placed our destiny in our own hands. But doctors are keen to wrest it back. Biology *is* destiny, and the test

61

of a real woman, at the end of the twentieth century, is the lengths
to which she will go – the indignities and ineffectual treatments
she will endure – in the hope, however vain, of conceiving a child.
Ecce ancilla medicorum.

I'm Gonna Make You A . . .

TOWARDS THE END of the 1840s, a politically turbulent decade which saw several European countries plunged into the revolutions of 1848, two significant cultural events took place in London. One was the formation, in 1848–9, of the artistic movement known as the Pre-Raphaelite Brotherhood; the other was the publication, in the winter of 1849, of Charlotte Brontë's novel *Shirley*. Neither was an overnight success, although the Pre-Raphaelites, initially greeted with scepticism, were soon championed by the influential critic John Ruskin and began to enjoy a degree of popularity which has not yet abated, judging by the frequency with which their images continue to adorn everything from postcards to book covers to chocolate boxes. There is an entire room of work by Dante Gabriel Rossetti, William Holman Hunt, John Everett Millais, Edward Burne-Jones, Arthur Hughes and their associates at the Tate Gallery in London, as well as significant collections in provincial museums like the Ashmolean in Oxford and the City Museum and Art Gallery, Birmingham. Many of their images, like Rossetti's *Proserpine*, are instantly recognisable to people who could name neither the pictures nor the artists, nor explain their allegorical meaning. Charlotte Brontë's novel, by contrast, has never been a favourite even among Brontë scholars, who have tended to regard its heroine, the heiress Shirley Keeldar, as too obviously idealised and surrounded by male characters who never really come to life. Set in what was then the recent past – the second decade of the nineteenth century – *Shirley* is about the conflict between modernising mill owners and the workers (Luddites) who correctly feared that the arrival of sophisticated weaving machines would destroy their jobs, a contest in which Charlotte's sympathies seem to have been divided. The story continually shifts focus away from the mills to Shirley and her rousing feminist declarations about a woman's role, suggesting that another kind of modernisation – how to update Victorian notions of femininity – was as much on its author's mind as its ostensible subject. Indeed, the novel's ideas about women are nothing short of revolutionary, prompting Charlotte's biographer Lyndall Gordon to describe Shirley as 'so much a forerunner of the feminist of the later twentieth century that it is hard to believe in her actual existence in 1811–12'. An orphan with a substantial fortune, Shirley directs her own financial affairs, proudly telling her timid (and anorexic) friend Caroline Helstone:

> Business! Really the word makes me conscious I am no longer a girl, but quite a woman and something more. I am an esquire: Shirley Keeldar, Esquire, ought to be my style and title. They gave me a man's name; I hold a man's position; it is enough to inspire me with a touch of manhood . . .

Lyndall Gordon characterises Shirley as 'a theoretic possibility: what a woman might be if she combined independence and means of her own with intellect', but there is an underlying uneasiness in the text. Can Shirley take on so many aspects of a man's role and remain a woman, even a completely new kind of woman? It is this anxiety, as much as Charlotte Brontë's inability to think beyond the 'standard Victorian marriage plot', which brings about the novel's unconvincing denouement: Shirley's marriage to the dreary tutor, Louis Moore, and her subsequent transformation into an anonymous entity identified only as 'Mrs Louis'. Yet while *Shirley* simultaneously demonstrates the range and limitations of its creator's imagination, it does at least try to come up with a new answer to the vexed question of what it might mean, in the middle of the nineteenth century, to be a woman. One of Shirley's most passionate outbursts is an attack on men's illusions about her sex, and the way they found expression in contemporary novels, plays and poetry. Although the novel looked backwards in terms of its setting, there is nothing historical or sentimental about Charlotte's vision; her grasp of the process by which male artists reinforced each other's prejudices is razor-sharp. Although the one branch of the arts she does not mention is painting, her speech could easily be read as an indictment of the way in which the Pre-Raphaelites fuelled each other's fantasies:

> If men could see us as we really are, they would be a little amazed; but the cleverest, the acutest men are often under an illusion about women: they do not read them in a true light; they misapprehend them, both for good and evil: their good woman is a queer thing, half doll, half angel; their bad woman almost always a fiend. Then to hear them fall into extasies with each other's creations, worshipping the heroine of such a poem – novel – drama, thinking it fine – divine! Fine and divine it may be, but often quite artificial – false as the rose in my best bonnet there. If I spoke all I think on this point; if I gave my real opinion of some first-rate female characters in first-rate works, where should I be? Dead under a cairn of avenging stones in half an hour.

Charlotte's characterisation of the ideal Victorian woman as 'half doll, half angel' has a deadly accuracy; the Pre-Raphaelites were consumed with nostalgia, hankering after an invented past which had very little to do with the lives of real women, especially the urban working class from which their models were drawn. The archetypal Pre-Raphaelite image, according to the art historian Jan Marsh, is 'a woman's face, set with large, lustrous eyes and surrounded by a mass of loose hair, looking soulfully out of the canvas'. Out of the canvas but not *at* the viewer; she lifts her eyes to the heavens, drops them in mournful supposition, gazes longingly at the horizon – anywhere, in fact, rather than make eye contact with the observer who occupies, roughly, the position adopted by the artist in the process of her creation. This is true of all the most celebrated Pre-Raphaelite paintings: not just *Proserpine* but *Regina Cordium, April Love, Beata Beatrix, King Cophetua and the Beggar-Maid, The Bridesmaid, Bocca Baciata, Convent Thoughts, The Awakening Conscience, Ophelia, Monna Vanna, Fazio's Mistress, La Belle Iseult, Sidonia von Bork*, *Astarte Syriaca*, even the wistful emigrant in *The Last of England*. (A rare exception is Ford Madox Brown's disturbing and unfinished canvas *Take Your Son, Sir!*, currently hanging in the Tate, which shows an ambiguous female figure, modelled on the artist's wife, offering her naked child to a man visible in the mirror behind her.) The Pre-Raphaelite painters based their careers, in fact, on producing idealised portraits of women in neo-classical or cod-medieval settings such as ramparts, bowers and glades. These rural idylls, and the nymphs who inhabited them, appealed to precisely that section of the middle class – prosperous, city-dwelling merchants – who had gained most from the industrialisation of English cities and the entry of women, *en masse*, into the workforce.

But Rossetti, Holman Hunt *et al*, did not content themselves, in Charlotte Brontë's phrase, with falling 'into extasies with each other's creations'. Instead, they consciously set out in search of attractive working-class girls to use as their models, enthusing over a 'find' like red-haired Lizzie Siddal or Emma Hill with her 'fine abundance of beautiful yellow hair the tint of harvest corn'. Several painters frequently shared the same model, passing her from studio to studio, and sometimes bed to bed; Emma Hill had been modelling for Ford Madox Brown for a couple of years when their illegitimate daughter Catherine was born in 1850. These affairs with young girls – they were more often than not teenagers when they caught someone's eye – were eventually to become as celebrated as the Pre-Raphaelites' canvases, as Jan Marsh observes:

> At another level, Pre-Raphaelitism evokes vivid, memorable anecdotes about the private lives of the painters – how the girl who posed for Millais' drowned Ophelia caught pneumonia, how Rossetti married his model and after her death dug up her coffin to retrieve his poems, how Holman Hunt fell for a ravishing slum girl and left her being educated while he went off to paint in the Holy Land.

These legends inevitably contain distortions: Lizzie Siddal caught a heavy cold, not pneumonia, when she lay in a tin bath full of water posing for *Ophelia* and the oil lamps placed underneath to keep her warm, unnoticed by Millais, went out. But Rossetti did reopen Lizzie's grave, seven years after her death in 1862, to retrieve the love poems he had buried with her in an excess of grief. (In a revealing detail, those present at the midnight exhumation put about the story that Lizzie's hair remained, against all expectation, as bright as ever. Fantasy was always preferable to reality, especially when faced with the unpleasant fact of decomposition.) Nor was Rossetti alone in marrying his model. William Morris courted and married Jane Burden, the daughter of a stablehand from Oxford, and reluctantly accepted her long extra-marital relationship with Rossetti, whose favourite model she became; Ford Madox Brown eventually contracted a secret marriage with Emma Hill, three years after their daughter was born. The Pre-Raphaelites shared, in other words, not just a set of high-minded ideals about painting but a Pygmalion fantasy about their ability to create the ideal woman in art *and* in life. The parallel with the Greek myth could hardly be more exact: just as the sculptor Pygmalion created his ideal woman, Galatea, from ivory and fell in love with her, the Pre-Raphaelites seem to have regarded working-class girls as convenient *tabulae rasae* on which, as men as well as artists, they could inscribe their notions of acceptable femininity. It is clear from their writings that they regarded this joint project not merely as transformational but as a rescue mission in which the girls were 'saved' from living conditions which, to the artists, appeared both shocking and alluring. Holman Hunt's account of the circumstances in which his teenage model Annie Miller was living, when he discovered her in a Chelsea slum in the early 1850s, is exceptionally revealing: Miller, whom he liked to believe he had saved from certain 'ruin', was 'without even the habits of cleanliness, living in the foulest of courts . . . allowed to prowl about the streets using the coarsest and filthiest language . . . in a state of the most absolute neglect and degradation'. The image is simultaneously feline and erotic; like Morris with Jane Burden, Holman Hunt set about educating his lovely primitive but, without Morris's egalitarian instincts, could not quite bring himself to marry her. In 1863, disillusioned with the artist, Miller finally married a Captain Thompson, cousin of Lord Ranelagh, turning herself, in Jan Marsh's words, into 'a striking example of a woman who had not fallen but risen'. Fanny Cornforth, by contrast, really did work as a prostitute before beginning her career as a Pre-Raphaelite model and sitting for works like *Fazio's Mistress*, in which Rossetti portrayed her in a sumptuous off-the-shoulder gown, plaiting her luxuriant hair. Although Fanny was Rossetti's long-term mistress, none of the Brothers was ever so rash as to consider her as a potential bride; her two spouses were, respectively, a mechanic and a bandsman, the latter nastily described by Rossetti's great friend Hall Caine as 'a misshapen German Jew'. There were limits, it seems, to how far the Pre-Raphaelites were prepared to go in indulging their fantasies about rehabilitating fallen women.

'What a stupendously beautiful creature I have found, by Jove! She's like a queen, magnificently tall, with a lovely figure, a stately neck, and a face full of the most delicate and finished modelling . . .' This, according to a later account by Rossetti's brother, was how Walter Deverell announced his discovery of Lizzie Siddal in 1849 to Dante Gabriel Rossetti and William Holman Hunt. On a visit with his mother to a milliner's shop in Cranborne Alley, off Leicester Square, Deverell spotted Lizzie, aged about twenty, working in a back room and instantly decided she had the look he wanted for the character of Viola in the scene from *Twelfth Night* he happened to be working on. He urged his mother to ask the owner of the shop for 'permission for her assistant to sit to him' and, in Jan Marsh's words, Siddal 'was successfully launched on a new career'. She had no sooner finished her assignment for Deverell than Holman Hunt used her for the figure of a woman bathing the face of a Christian missionary in a large historical painting for which he had had trouble finding suitable models. More work flowed in, with Lizzie employed to sit for Holman Hunt's *Valentine Rescuing Sylvia* and Rossetti's *Rossovestita*. Within two years of her discovery, Siddal was well on her way to becoming the first Pre-Raphaelite star, even if no one outside the Brotherhood and their circle actually knew her name.

Almost 150 years later, in 1987, an almost identical scene to the one in Cranborne Alley was played out in the ultra-modern setting

of a Düsseldorf disco. Michel Levaton, a French clothing manufac-
turer who had recently set up Metropolitan Models, a company
whose *raison d'être* was spotting new faces for modelling agencies
and photographers, noticed a pretty blonde schoolgirl who had
the look he was seeking and approached her on the dance-floor.
'You look really good,' he told her. 'Do you want to be a model?'
The girl, who was seventeen, was naturally suspicious. 'You know
how the French are,' she said later. 'I kept dancing. He kept trying
to speak to me. I told him to stop bothering me. So he went to
talk with my friends.' Eventually, worn down by his persistence,
she gave him her parents' phone number. As in Walter Deverell's
dealings with Siddal, the introduction of a parental go-between
was crucial; Levaton dialled the number he had been given,
arranged lunch with the girl's father and mother, and another
career was launched. Her first assignments, while she was still at
school, included an advert for Revlon cosmetics and a cover for
Elle; in 1993 she signed a $6 million contract with Revlon and
was taken up by the German designer Karl Lagerfeld, who made
her the star of his shows in Paris for the prestigious French house
of Chanel. Within six years, Claudia Schiffer had gone from the
obscurity of a Rheinberg high school to a position as the world's
highest-earning model.

Schiffer's story isn't quite rags-to-riches and her earning power
far exceeds the pittance made by her Victorian predecessors,
even if their faces were, in their own context, almost as well
known. But her career trajectory, from teenage *ingénue* to female
icon in a few short years, has striking parallels with what
happened to the Pre-Raphaelite women. So do those of the
British supermodels Naomi Campbell and Kate Moss. Campbell,
who was born in suburban Streatham in 1970, attended stage
school but was talent-spotted during a shopping trip to Covent
Garden; she was modelling for *Elle* at fifteen and the first black
model to appear on the covers of French and British *Vogue*.
Moss was discovered at Kennedy Airport, New York, in 1988
while her father tried to get standby seats on a flight back
to London. Still only fourteen, Moss's modelling career took
off because of the persistence of the founder of the Storm
agency, who shrugged off the initially puzzled reactions to Moss's

waif-like appearance and insisted: 'I'm going to make you a star.'

That these contemporary 'discovery' narratives contain elements of the tired old Pygmalion fantasy is illustrated by the story of Aline Wermelinger, a Brazilian schoolgirl spotted in 1992 by a scout from the Elite modelling agency in New York. Wermelinger was only sixteen when she got through to the finals of the Look of the Year contest, a break which led to a meeting with the agency's founder, the legendary – in fashion circles at least – John Casablancas. Casablancas, who was in his late forties, twice divorced and a former boyfriend of the model Stephanie Seymour, was entranced by the the the young newcomer, who declared that her favourite book was the Bible, and went to Brazil to meet her parents. 'I saw her family and her house, and I asked permission to marry her,' he said, adding: 'I loved the values she brought.' The couple's wedding coincided with Wermelinger's retirement from her scarcely launched career 'to tend to his needs full-time', thus completing her transformation from model to model wife in record time. Other women, particularly those with brighter prospects – Casablancas's professional assessment of his bride was that there was something not quite right about her nose – are more hard-headed. Kate Moss's big break was a topless photo shoot with the pop star Marky Mark for Calvin Klein, a blurring of the line between 'respectable' exposure of the body and soft porn which drew criticism from Claudia Schiffer. Moss was undaunted. 'That's how [Schiffer] made her fortune,' she retorted. 'She's got an amazing body and big tits. She sold her body like I sold mine.'

But it isn't just a question of bodies. What Schiffer, Campbell and Moss have in common, in spite of their very different physiques, is an ability to offer their perfect – and perfectly blank – faces as a canvas on which all kinds of fantasies can be written. Unlike their Victorian predecessors, they have to create that empty screen themselves; whatever joy or distress they happen to be feeling has to be hidden from the camera's piercing eye. Our impressions of the Pre-Raphaelite women are mediated through the poses and expressions selected for them by their artist lovers, so much so that their faces, soulful and

70

yearning at first sight, tell us nothing about their true feelings, even though we know sufficient biographical details to guess that they were frequently dissatisfied, to say the very least, with their lot: Burden's marriage to Morris made them both miserable, Siddal was addicted to laudanum and died of an overdose at the age of thirty-two, Cornforth was 'shattered' by Rossetti's marriage to Siddal. Almost always painted in character, it is a striking fact that their facial expressions are more or less interchangeable from picture to picture, making an image like the *Mona Lisa* appear positively voluble by comparison. But it would be a mistake to think that, just because Campbell, Moss and Schiffer appear to us in photographic images instead of through the indirect medium of paint, our knowledge of them is correspondingly more authentic. What we recognise, on fashion posters and magazine covers, is merely a collection of features, carefully ordered into that self-effacing blandness which is the supermodels' prime asset; all that has changed is the amount of money they can earn – an estimated $12 million a year in the case of Schiffer – and the way in which they have become names in their own right, for the most part much better known than the talent scouts, photographers and couturiers who kick-started their careers.

It is as if Lizzie Siddal had become more famous, in her day, than Dante Gabriel Rossetti – an absurd suggestion even though she was, as it happens, a moderately talented painter in her own right. Lizzie, Annie, Emma, Fanny and Jane never became household names like Naomi, Kate, Cindy, Christy and Claudia. Yet even in the case of the supermodels, the little-girl names by which they are known are telling. Models have, in effect, grown up in terms of business acumen but not in public perception; if anything, their enhanced earning power has been accompanied by a visual and cultural relegation from the realm of adult women. A striking example of this tendency to treat them as fractious children was the public dressing-down administered to Schiffer in the summer of 1996 by, among others, her erstwhile mentor Karl Lagerfeld. Lagerfeld dismissed the 26-year-old Schiffer as past her sell-by date, too bland for anything but product promotion, yet only a couple of years previously her lack of memorable features – she does not even have Cindy Crawford's famous facial mole –

was winning her plaudits as the most beautiful 'girl' in the world. When an obviously hurt Schiffer responded by announcing her retirement from modelling, it was hard not to sympathise; her doll-like prettiness and tousled blonde hair had not altered one jot, so it was far from obvious why Lagerfeld had decreed she was no longer up to the job. Schiffer was being denounced, in effect, for precisely that aspect of her appearance which was once her selling point while her peers, the inscrutable Moss and the habitually expressionless Campbell, were as much in demand as ever, giving the lie to any suggestion that liveliness and bags of character were suddenly the *sine qua non* of success as a top model.

The sequel to this episode, a few months later at the Paris collections, was both painful and instructive. Schiffer not only agreed to appear at Lagerfeld's show for Chanel but allowed him to humiliate her by sending her on to the catwalk in a ludicrous black wig and clear plastic shoes with heels so high that, had she not been carried past the expectant fashion journalists on an airline-style conveyor belt, she would almost certainly have toppled over. Schiffer's consolation, if she needed one, was that Lagerfeld handed out much the same treatment to Campbell, Moss and Stella Tennant. All four women looked, according to one report, 'like dummies in a department store window as an 80ft moving walkway whisked them past an amused audience'. Yet none of them showed her feelings in anything other than compliant smiles, even though Campbell in particular has a fearsome reputation, behind the scenes, for losing her temper. Supermodels are, of course, *paid* not to react, no matter how many slights and affronts are offered to them; what is striking about the terms of their job is that, for all its glamour, it frequently requires them to parade in outfits which poke fun at rather than enhance their bodies and faces. This marks a significant break with the past, for while the Pre-Raphaelite women almost always posed in the costumes of another era, the sumptuous silks and glowing velvets which were an integral part of the movement's nostalgic fantasies about women, they were never required to look ridiculous. Indeed, while the relation between the Brotherhood and their models was blatantly unequal, an eroticised version of the master–servant connection, today's supermodels are trapped in an even more sinister association with some of the men – and most top-flight couturiers, the Lagerfelds, Versaces and Valentinos of this world, *are* men – who employ them.

Absurd wigs, crippling shoes, torn dresses, puffball skirts, schoolgirl outfits, the baby doll look known as *Kinderwhore* – these perennial features of the spring and autumn collections speak volumes about their designers' unconscious (for the most part) urges to control beautiful women and cut them down to size. Yet they are regularly explained away by a compliant press as whims or jokes, so much so that a textbook example of the most blatant misogyny can easily masquerade as the cutting edge of fashion. When 27-year-old Lee Alexander McQueen became the idol of style journalists in the autumn of 1996, taking over from another British designer, the flamboyant John Galliano, at the patrician house of Givenchy, pundits enthused that 'he has done more to put our beleaguered fashion industry back on the international map than any other designer'. McQueen was suddenly the toast of London and Paris, even though his freakish ideas about women were boldly and unashamedly exposed in the clothes his models were required to wear. Fashion writers concentrated instead on his working-class background and lack of experience, with even Susannah Frankel in the *Guardian* acknowledging the sense of unease created by his clothes and dismissing it in the same breath:

> While [McQueen] is certainly the most talented designer to come out of London since Galliano, he has only designed eight collections (at Givenchy he would be responsible for 10 a year), taking their often twisted inspiration from subjects as unpalatable as rape, car crash and famine victims. In the highland rape [sic] collection, the final decorative touch was tampon strings dangling from crotches of McQueen's signature bumster trousers. Not only is he far from experienced, his ideology is a million miles from that of the moneyed and mannered couture customer for whom he will be catering.

In his brief career, McQueen has managed to feature models

in frogged greatcoats with essential pieces hacked off to reveal bedraggled lace undergarments, like aristocratic rape victims trailing in the wake of a victorious army. His most notorious pre-Givenchy jape consisted of sending a black model on to the catwalk in manacles, her wrists and ankles attached to a rusty frame which meant she could hardly walk. Another 'joke', or an image which excites by exploiting associations between racial and sexual bondage? McQueen's admirers cite in his defence a previous prank, this time perpetrated on the Prince of Wales, during the time the designer worked as an apprentice at the royal tailors, Anderson & Sheppard, in London. 'Without him knowing it', McQueen boasted later, 'the Prince of Wales has worn a jacket with "I'm a cunt" written on the front of it.' For his fans, it was a typically iconoclastic gesture from an East End lad whose motivation is a coarse sense of humour rather than anything more ominous. It certainly didn't prevent his receiving the accolade, only a week after his appointment at Givenchy, of being named British designer of the year for 1996.

But why is the joke in *haute couture*, with rare exceptions like McQueen's childish trick on the Prince of Wales, almost always at the expense of women? The same accusation could be made against some female designers, notably Vivienne Westwood, whose stunts in recent years have ranged from an attempt to reintroduce that ghastly *fin de siècle* deformity, the bustle, to creating the twelve-inch platform soles which famously tripped up Naomi Campbell. Yet Westwood's ambiguity towards the female body seems rooted in feelings about her own anatomy; she constantly breaks taboos, including the powerful one which forbids older women to expose their bodies – she has appeared in public in one of her own creations, a transparent dress defiantly worn without underwear – and as often as not her own person is the subject of the experiment. Lagerfeld's double humiliation of Schiffer, by contrast, suggests neither a joke nor an experiment but some form of power struggle, as does McQueen's insistent linking of women's bodies with blood, suffering and sexual violence. Like the Pre-Raphaelite painters, both men display a need to dominate the women whose beauty they depend upon for their livelihood; unlike them – Lagerfeld and McQueen are gay – the urge cannot relieve itself through the traditional route of erotic mastery. Instead, it expresses itself in an impulse to reduce the women's status by treating them as children, victims or puppets; it is surely no accident that McQueen's spring/summer collection for 1997 was called *La Poupée* and required the models at his show to parade as stiffly and awkwardly as dolls.

Similar impulses can be traced right across the fashion industry, although they are seldom frankly acknowledged. A rare exception was an issue of the American magazine *Vanity Fair* in the spring of 1995 which began unremarkably with a cover showing not professional models but film stars: Uma Thurman and Nicole Kidman in their undies, a Donna Karan bodysuit and a black Dolce e Gabbana corset dress respectively, while another film star, Jennifer Jason Leigh, crouched on the floor beside them in a black high-waisted bra and shorts which resembled an old-fashioned girdle. Unusually, the cover folded out into a three-page spread which featured seven more actresses in bras, corsets and basques: nothing more, at first sight, than evidence of the magazine's sycophancy, under the editorship of Graydon Carter, towards the West Coast, and of its habit of shamelessly exploiting the female body to shift copies. But the overall message was much more insidious. On the reverse of the fold-out cover was a promotion of British fashion showing clothes by top names such as Rifat Ozbek, John Galliano, Liza Bruce and Paul Smith. And if the actresses on the cover were almost too perfect to be real women, the models in the Brit fashion spread took the atmosphere of unreality even further; they were not women at all but dolls, Barbie dolls. As the copy explained: 'The most Drop-Dead Glam Girl is in town! And the Best of British Designers are all begging for her body.'

Barbie was certainly a cheaper option for the advertisers than British supermodels like Campbell and Moss, the obvious choice for a feature on home-grown fashion. But the spread conveyed a more disturbing message than the superficial one that the top catwalk models were in danger of pricing themselves out of the market. The implication was not so much that women and dolls were interchangeable but that Barbie, with her moulded plastic breasts, tiny waist and pert bottom, represented the ideal female figure at the end of the twentieth century. If Charlotte Bronte believed that Victorian men were in love with 'a queer thing, half doll, half angel', she could scarcely have imagined that, 150 years on, things would have got significantly worse. But we live in an age when Proserpine has dwindled into Barbie, and even the blandest type of female beauty is being shouldered aside in favour of the superior attractions of a lump of guaranteed, all-American, one hundred per cent plastic.

Part II

Night Mares

The Selfish Jean

HOLD THE FRONT page: women have stopped having babies! Not all of them, but enough to make people sit up and take notice. And we're not talking about maiden aunts or women whose fiancés died tragically in the war. (Which war? When I was at school in the 1960s, we were always rather vague about the conflict in which the prospective bridegrooms of our unmarried teachers were assumed to have perished.) No, the hot news is that one in five women in developed countries like Britain are living out their adult lives without bearing a child. This is, we are told, a bad thing. Newspaper columns bulge pregnantly with agonised commentaries on this 'startling statistic', on the tragedy of women who are 'devastated to find they have waited too long', on the social consequences of a generation of childless oldies with no one to look after them in their declining years. Women are being forced to choose, columnists and feature writers warn, between careers and babies; women without children talk apologetically about what they have given up, about their regret that the right man never came along or the demands of jobs which made motherhood impossible for them. You can't have it all, newspaper columnists observe gleefully, pitying the thirty-something career women who have nothing to look forward to except a lonely old age in a home for the elderly, sitting unnoticed in a corner as their more fortunate neighbours romp with grandchildren and great-grandchildren.

But what's this? As the birth rate in Britain and other European countries drops below the replacement level of 2.1 births per woman, it's becoming apparent that this is not the whole story. In Austria, Belgium, Switzerland and West Germany, the birth rate is at an unprecedented low of between 1.5 and 1.4. In traditionally Catholic countries like Italy and Spain, it is even lower, at 1.3. These figures cannot be explained solely as evidence that a generation of women is reluctantly giving up motherhood for the sake of their careers. Some of them, it is clear, are choosing not to have children for no other reason than that *they don't want them*. It's a revolution in thinking as profound, in its own way, as Galileo's announcement in 1632 that the earth revolves around the sun, a discovery which landed him before the Inquisition on trial for heresy. For what the figures signal is the demise of an equally cherished myth, this time the one that insists on the existence of a universal maternal instinct.

For centuries, childlessness in women was a curse, a condition aspired to only by a handful of nuns, saints and female monarchs who feared the dilution of power attendant on marriage and the physical processes of pregnancy. This was the case even though childbirth was at best painful and at worst fatal; the poignant portraits of aristocratic women by Renaissance masters in the fifteenth century frequently record lives cut short, following a familiar pattern of arranged marriage, often to a much older man, numerous pregnancies in quick succession and then premature death. Battista Sforza sat for Piero della Francesca in 1465, along with her husband Count Federigo da Montefeltro; seven years later, in 1472, she was dead. She had just given birth to her first son and fifth child. Yet women everywhere dreaded the discovery that they were 'barren', a baleful adjective which appears over and over again in the Authorised Version of the Bible. Even the most powerful woman of her day, Elizabeth I, reacted bitterly when she heard that her political rival had just given birth to a boy. 'The queen of Scots is this day leichter of a fair son, and I am but a barren stock,' she exclaimed.

In this context the proposition that, given the choice, some women would prefer *not* to have children, was virtually unthinkable. Without reliable methods of contraception, the vast majority could and did have them as a matter of course. Women who couldn't conceive were pitied and showered with advice, emphasising both their private sense of failure and the primacy of motherhood as a woman's destiny. Their plight was social as well as personal, as we can see from the extraordinary and revealing letters exchanged in the late fourteenth century by a childless couple who lived in the Tuscan city of Prato, Francesco di Marco Datini and his wife Margherita di Domenico Bandini. The letters expose not just their increasing desperation and eventual estrangement as Margherita failed to conceive but the lengths they went to in a fruitless attempt to overcome the problem: prayers, a consultation with the Pope's doctor, folk remedies – a foul-smelling poultice placed on the stomach – and superstitious rituals suggested to Francesco by the wife of a family friend:

> She says it is to be girded on by a boy who is still a virgin, saying first three Our Fathers and Hail Marys in honour of God and the Holy Trinity and St Catherine; and the letters written on the belt are to be placed on the belly, on the naked flesh . . .

There is no reason to doubt the anguish of women like Margherita, who entered dynastic unions with much older men and then discovered that they were unable to achieve either the heirs their husbands required or the companionship with their children which they looked forward to when they married. Apart from anything else, with other occupations closed to women, they found themselves at a loose end – and, if their relatives were unkind, the butt of reproaches. Pregnancy was, though, for the vast majority of the female population, impossible to avoid, and it was perhaps inevitable that what most women did inevitably became confused with what they *wanted* to do – function elided with choice, we might say – so that the myth of a universal maternal instinct was born. So unquestioned was it that even the great birth control pioneers of the early twentieth century concerned themselves with regulating the *number* of children individual women gave birth to rather than the heretic notion that contraception might give them the choice not to have any at all. 'A family of healthy happy children should be the joy of every pair of married lovers,' Marie Stopes asserted confidently in 1918 at the beginning of *Wise Parenthood*, her 'treatise on birth control for married people'. Stopes was worried that 'babies come in general too quickly for the resources of most, and particularly of city-dwelling, families, and the parents as well as the children consequently suffer'. She certainly wasn't in the business of providing contraception for unmarried couples or teenage girls, an issue that has caused fierce debates in recent decades, and like many social welfare campaigners of her generation, her project was unashamedly eugenecist. (*Wise Parenthood* is dedicated 'to all those who wish to see our race grow in strength and beauty'.)

It was not until the 1960s, when a reinvigorated women's movement on both sides of the Atlantic began to look at issues around sexuality and reproduction in a new and radical light, that the idea that some women might not want children began to be voiced even in a hesitant way. The founding feminist text on women's sexual lives, *Our Bodies Ourselves*, published by the Boston Women's Health Book Collective in 1971, hedged its short section on voluntary childlessness with nervous qualifiers: 'Although our culture is *rather resistant* to the image of the non-nurturant woman, *some of us* feel we are not interested or cut out to be mothers' [my italics]. For the American feminist writer Judith Arcana, in *Our Mothers' Daughters*, not having children was 'that difficult minority decision'. Ellen Peck, in a defensive and badly written book called *The Baby Trap*, felt she had to justify her own decision not to give birth by expounding at length on her devotion to travel, art and culture. What women found almost impossible to say, even in the heady days of the early 1970s, was that they simply did not want children. This was so much the case that the vast social change already beginning to get under way, with the arrival of the oral contraceptive pill, happened furtively and took almost everyone by surprise. Not only did the birth rate decline in affluent Western countries – even in the United States, where the change has been slower, it was hovering around the replacement level of two births per woman by 1992 – but the proportion of women living out their their reproductive years without ever giving birth began to rise rapidly. The figure had always been higher than most people appreciated: 13 per cent of women born in England and Wales in 1947, for instance, were still childless at the age of forty in 1987. But, according to a recent publication by the government's Central Statistical

Office, 'this proportion has increased sharply over time and it is now expected that over a fifth of women born in 1967 will still be childless when they reach 40'. How far this is the result of a conscious decision on the part of women, rather than accident or the absence of a partner, is demonstrated by another statistic from the British government's General Household Survey: the number of women aged sixteen to forty-nine who said they expected to remain childless doubled between 1986 and 1991, from 5 per cent to 10 per cent.

So what happened? Is there something radically different about women born after the Second World War, something that marks them out from every other generation that has gone before? Instead of addressing this fascinating question, and relating it to other developments like access to education and employment and the wide availability of the contraceptive pill, reactions to the trend have been almost wholly negative. In a typical feature in April 1995 commenting on the latest statistics, the *Independent* asked anxiously whether society needs to 'remould the traditional role of motherhood to improve its attractiveness'. A front-page article in the *Guardian* in June 1996 warned that 'the birth rate is already below the level necessary to replenish the population' and quoted a statistician at the Office for National Statistics (ONS) who said: 'It is a problem. We are likely to to have a population more heavily weighted towards the elderly.' The ONS predicted in 1996 that Britain's population would begin to fall in 2025 for the first time since the Black Death in the middle of the fourteenth century, unintentionally characterising voluntary childlessness as a threat to humanity on the scale of a medieval plague. (I have never seen comparable tables or articles about voluntarily childless *men*, a group which certainly exists but which seems thus far to have escaped the attentions of both population experts and feature writers alike.)

There is an element of *fin de siècle* and indeed millennarian scaremongering in such comparisons, and it's striking that they are always made without context. Since the Second World War, the fear that has stalked the planet has been *over* population, and the prospect of a declining birth rate in the developed world might be seen as a modest but welcome contribution to dealing with this increasingly urgent problem. The earth's population has been increasing at a daunting rate, placing pressure on finite resources such as land, food, water, oil and gas; in the early 1990s it stood at 5.42 billion, with a 'doubling time' – at present rates of growth – of only forty-one years. At the same time, it was estimated that even with present low fertility rates, the British population would show a modest *increase*, from 57.8 million to 61 million, by the year 2025. Looked at globally, population statistics usually produce grave anxiety about sustainable development, as in this assessment by Professor Edward O. Wilson of Harvard University:

> The raging monster upon the land is population growth. In its presence, sustainability is but a fragile theoretical construct. To say, as many do, that the difficulties of nations are due not to people but to poor ideology or land-use management is sophistic. If Bangladesh had 10 million inhabitants instead of 115 million, its impoverished people could live on prosperous farms away from the dangerous floodplains midst a natural and stable upland environment . . . If all nations held the same number of people per square kilometer, they would converge in quality of life to Bangladesh rather than the Netherlands or Japan, and their irreplaceable natural resources would soon join the seven wonders of the world as scattered vestiges of an ancient history.

Wilson's view may be unduly pessimistic, but a dispassionate observer would be hard pressed to identify population *decline* rather than uncontrolled increase as the most pressing problem the world faces. So why is it that, at the very moment we have begun to hear good news about a slowdown in the birth rate in Western Europe, statisticians and journalists are conjuring up a doomsday scenario comparable with natural disasters like the Black Death? That pestilence, it is worth recalling here, carried off something like a third of the populations of those European countries unfortunate enough to be affected by it in the plague year of 1348. The prospect of one woman in five deciding not to have children is in no way equivalent in its effect, or indeed in terms of human suffering, to the ravages of a pandemic disease;

the anxieties expressed about the trend are so alarmist, and so transparently unreal, as to suggest that something else is going on which has not as yet been openly acknowledged.

What might that be? The questions of class and race cannot be discounted, for at least some of the apprehensions about falling birth rates in developed countries are prompted by the prospect that the wrong kind of people – working-class mothers or women in Third World countries – will carry on breeding unchecked. (This perpetual anxiety of the middle and upper classes can be traced back at least as far as Roman times.) In his authoritative text *Population Geography*, Huw Jones points out that successive governments in Western Europe have shown less concern about sub-replacement levels of fertility in the 1970s and 1980s than their predecessors did about a similar trend in the 1930s. 'Technological advances in armaments, manufacturing production and services have undermined the crude size role of military and labour manpower, so that the traditional view of a country's security, economic power and international prestige being a function of its population size has faded,' he writes. (The one exception, apparently, is France.) What this means is that Western governments no longer rely on population size as a virility symbol, although they do worry about the economic impact of an ageing population. Yet even this fear, says Jones, 'is often overstated' and an elderly population 'does level off under conditions of stable fertility'.

There is, in other words, a lot less cause for alarm about the West's low birth rate than you would imagine from reading reports of the trend in newspapers. But that is far from being the whole story. When an individual woman says she doesn't want to have children, she immediately encounters a spectrum of hostile reactions ranging from disbelief ('you'll change your mind when you're older') to condescension ('you don't know what you're missing'), from accusations of solipsism ('have you *always* been so selfish?') to full-frontal assaults on her femininity ('what's *wrong* with you?'). I can speak with some authority on this subject because I am one of those women; I have no idea whether I am fertile, sub-fertile or incapable of conceiving, for I have never been interested enough to find out. If I have a biological clock, it must be silent and digital, for I have never heard it tick, even though I am (at the time of writing) in my early forties. Over the years, however, I have become wearily familiar with all the responses outlined above, and with some bizarre variants such as 'How dare you not have children when other women are desperate to get pregnant?' Equally popular is a testy demand that I should lie about my reason for not having children, that I should hint at lengthy and unsuccessful courses of fertility treatment, thereby emphasising the point that childlessness is just about acceptable for a woman as long as it isn't voluntary. Obviously I could lower my eyes, take out a handkerchief and pretend that I'm resigned to my barren state. Or I could go along with the line of a well-meaning friend who said she admired my decision not to have children because it was one of the most difficult a woman could make. But it isn't, not for me. I grew up not wanting children in the same way that I didn't aspire to be an airline pilot or a nuclear physicist; there was no painful soul-searching or introspection, just a useful and early piece of self-knowledge I have always trusted and acted upon.

On its own, this lack of interest in having children might not have equipped me to withstand the astonishing degree of social pressure on women to conform to a single pattern. The deciding factor was knowing from an early age exactly what I did want, that I was absolutely impassioned about being a writer. It's not that I thought writing and motherhood were incompatible, just that having such a fierce ambition threw into shadow all the things – including having children – that I didn't want to do. I have never felt the need to apologise for this. I didn't enjoy being a child, a point I make when people accuse me of not realising what I'm missing; I was one for what seemed a maddeningly long time, about a third of my life so far, and leaving behind that infantile and adolescent world was a tremendous relief. I put away childish things gladly, to put my own gloss on St Paul, and I don't want to re-encounter them in surrogate form in the role of somebody else's parent. This is not to devalue motherhood, not for those who want to do it and who delight, as I don't, in the company of small children. What I do insist on is the right to be different without being punished or pitied, a right men take for granted.

In case you think I'm exaggerating the hostility that women like myself routinely encounter, here is a piece of writing – it's actually a radio review from the *Independent* – which displays some of the reactions I've been talking about:

The thing that people without children never seem to appreciate is the full-blooded, gutsy thrills involved in rearing the next generation. 'Without Issue', a feature on Radio 4 last night about why women choose not to have children, opened with a stereotypically cute little montage of childhood sounds – a tinkling musical box and a lisping voice reciting a nursery rhyme . . .

If infancy really was as icky as it sounded there, childlessness ought not to be so much an option as a legal obligation. But to have children is not to cut yourself off from the dirt and squalor and moral depravity of everyday life; it's to be thrust into a new world of primal emotion, of instinctive violence unconstrained by fear or scruple. One male interviewee on 'Without Issue' complained that parents he knew seemed to use children as an excuse not to do interesting and exciting things. The poor sap: sure, whitewater rafting may offer more of a physical challenge than putting a pair of dungarees on a protesting two-year-old; but it's unlikely to offer a more intense emotional experience. Children are a test of character more exacting than anything you're likely to encounter outside Homer.

Speaking – as you've probably deduced – as a parent, I've always thought that not having children was a perfectly reasonable option. 'Without Issue' left me less sympathetic. Early on, one woman complained that people told her not having children was selfish, and Liz Lochhead, who linked the interviews with a polemical commentary, took her side: after a succession of interviewees talked about how they wanted their sleep, and wanted money, and didn't want the responsibility, she asked whether it would be kind for such people to have offspring.

It's a fair point; all the same, it was hard not to be struck by the rampant individualism on display here – epitomised by Christina Dodwell, who talked about her ideal moments on top of a mountain with virtually no human life for miles. Perhaps they didn't realise it, but these people came across as devout Thatcherites, dedicated to the belief that there's no such thing as society.

As it happens, I am the interviewee singled out by the author of the piece (a journalist named Robert Hanks) in his third paragraph. To demonstrate that Hanks is far from alone in his casual assumption of moral superiority over childless people, here is the final paragraph of a letter sent to the *Guardian* by a female reader who was incensed by an article I wrote about choosing not to have children:

> Just one thing – when my time comes to leave this world (not too far distant I guess) I'll look at my grandchildren and feel that I have done something to contribute to things . . . Perhaps having written a few words on a word processor, paper, what have you, gives one the same feeling of achievement? I shall never know.

Articles and letters like the ones I've just quoted reveal the hopeless confusion which surrounds the subject of voluntary childlessness. If having children and grandchildren is so universally rewarding, why is it *selfish* to deny oneself the pleasure of parenthood? If, on the other hand, bringing up children is as arduous a task as Hanks suggests, why does he feel sorry for people who don't do it? But logic doesn't have much place in this debate – it's actually more of a slanging match, with most of the insults flying in one direction – because it very quickly becomes bogged down around this single issue of altruism. This is not surprising, given that the adulation of motherhood, especially as encouraged by the Christian churches, can be understood as a *quid pro quo* for undertaking what were, for most of recorded history, the dangerous activities of pregnancy and childbirth; even now, in Italy, the Catholic Church is considering the beatification of a woman who died after refusing cancer treatment which would endanger her unborn child. Until very recently, the only practical escape route for women who wished to avoid repeated pregnancies was the cloister; significantly, they were required to undertake an alternative form of altruistic surrender, giving up both the world and sexual pleasure. (St Catherine of Siena, according to historians, 'received visions which led her to vow her virginity to Jesus Christ' and in doing so escaped her mother's exhausting fate of producing more than twenty children. Catherine's persistent and well-documented anorexia, one of whose effects is to prevent menstruation, may have been another unconscious strategy to avoid motherhood. It is a striking fact that she shared the condition with other religious women of the period, most of them far less celebrated but equally resistant to self-nourishment and female maturity.) In other words, a woman who wanted to remain childless had to atone through another, very public act of self-denial. Those twentieth-century women like myself who choose not to have children, yet continue to enjoy sexual relations with men, fail on both counts.

Women are not supposed to want things *for themselves*, and an admission that an individual woman doesn't yearn to be a mother automatically prompts accusations of unbridled hedonism. It is tempting to discern old stereotypes lurking behind this discussion, in that the degree of anger and contempt showered on childless women is so disproportionate as to suggest that a refusal of the category of mother automatically displaces them into that of whore. As always, the process of binary opposition works to bathe one of two alternatives, mothers in this instance, in a beatific glow; mother love still has an iconic place in Western culture, in theory if not reality, to a point where the true nature of the relationship is hardly ever examined. This is that mothers (and many fathers) have a narcissistic investment in their children which sanctions forms of behaviour which, to an outside observer, are quite clearly motivated by self-interest or the narrow interests of the family group. This is not so much a criticism as a recognition that it is *parents* who most obviously exemplify Margaret Thatcher's dictum that there is no such thing as society, a philosophy which grants unique privileges to the family and plays down or even denies the existence of common interests between people who are *not* related. The gap between theory and practice is often acute, as was revealed when the leader of the then Opposition, Tony Blair, and his front bench colleague Harriet Harman had to make decisions about where their elder children should be educated. Instead of sending them to local state schools, and working to raise standards for the benefit of *all* the pupils there, both politicians arranged for their children to attend selective schools – on the other side of London in Blair's case – whose very existence stands in opposition to their party's education policy. This is a form of self-interest which dresses itself up as altruism – 'I don't want my children to suffer for my beliefs' – but is quite clearly tribal in origin, granting privileges to blood ties over the welfare of society in general. Equally telling are some of the reasons people give for deciding to have children in the first place: to save a failing marriage, to perpetuate their genes, so they will have someone to look after them in their old age. All this goes to show that the charge of solipsism can just as easily be laid at the door of parents as of those who have chosen not to take this route.

Once this aspect of the debate is seen as the blind alley it really is, we arrive at a situation in which the *real* objection to women who decide not to have children can be unmasked. In fact Robert Hanks has already given it away in his article when he uses the pejorative term 'rampant individualism': if women don't conform to the expected pattern – if, crucially, they aren't all looking after children for at least part of their adult lives – what else might they do? Pursue their own interests? Compete with men? There is a telling historical parallel here: in the second half of the nineteenth century, when the number of single women in the British population began to outstrip the pool of men available for marriage, a journalist called William R. Greg wrote an essay in the *Westminster Review* entitled 'Why Are Women Redundant?' Worried that their dissatisfaction might be the engine for social and political reform, Greg pointed out the 'enormous and increasing number of single women in the nation, a number quite disproportionate and quite abnormal; a number which positively and relatively is indicative of an unwholesome social state'. Unable to take on the 'natural duties and labours of wives and mothers', these surplus women were being forced to 'carve out artificial and painfully-sought occupations for themselves' instead of taking on the traditional women's role of 'completing, sweetening, and embellishing the existence of others'. (There's that famous female altruism again.) Greg's innovative solution was to ship these unwanted spinsters out to the Colonies, where there were plenty of men who needed wives, housekeepers and mothers for their children; what really alarmed him was the prospect that demographic pressure might encourage women to demand access to other walks of life, such as the professions. And, of course, he was right. The feminist writer Jessie Boucherett, in an essay entitled 'How to Provide for Superfluous Women', suggested that single women should be allowed 'to engage freely in all occupations suited to their strength ... thus converting them into useful members of society'.

While significant differences exist between the final decades of the nineteenth and twentieth centuries, the panic – I do not think it is too strong a word – in recent years over voluntary childlessness has striking echoes of the anxieties of the earlier period. For centuries, it could be safely assumed that the vast majority of women would spend the bulk of their pre-menopausal lives pregnant or bringing up children. This was, in effect, a highly efficient way of confining them to the domestic sphere. Even today, as we approach the third millennium, it is still widely assumed that the working patterns of most women will be different from those of men: interrupted by maternity leave and career breaks, disqualified for promotion by the need to job-share or work part-time. Working mothers have argued, quite rightly, that employment patterns should change to suit *their* needs instead of forcing them to work what is in effect a double shift; in some industries and occupations, this has already happened to some extent. But what is the effect if a fifth of the female population decides not to take this route?

The consequences are far-reaching. Some women are already able to compete with men in the employment market on completely equal terms, but this is not even the half of it. What has been demolished is nothing less than the comfortable assumption that women can be treated, as they have been from time immemorial, as a single homogeneous class. I have always been puzzled by the extent to which it is assumed that every woman in the world, regardless of her race or class or education or personality, wants to do exactly the same thing. Not any more. Birth statistics and population tables may not appear exciting at first glance, but their message, in this instance, is both consistent and revolutionary. All women are *not* the same. This is good news. It makes life more interesting. Get used to it.

The Lady Vanishes

THERE IS A scene near the beginning of *Double Indemnity* when Fred MacMurray meets Barbara Stanwyck for the first time, calling unannounced at her home in a suburb of San Francisco in the hope of persuading her to renew her husband's motor insurance with his company. MacMurray is announced by the maid and Stanwyck appears at the top of the stairs, dressed only in a bath towel and setting the stage for one of those rapid-fire exchanges of double entendres so characteristic of *film noir*. Once she returns, still buttoning her dress, the conversation moves quickly from motor to accident insurance, with Stanwyck's protestations of anxiety about her husband's dangerous job in the oil industry conveying precisely the opposite of her actual words, even to a character as slow-witted as MacMurray's insurance agent Walter Neff. MacMurray makes an inept play for Stanwyck and she shows him the door, accusing him of driving too fast in a built-up area, but what is really going on between them is revealed in a series of smouldering glances. The audience is left in no doubt that MacMurray will be back, or that Stanwyck will sucker him into killing her husband. This is, after all, a suburban housewife who is prepared to greet a total stranger half-dressed and wearing *an ankle chain*, even in 1944.

According to the influential American film critic Pauline Kael, the type of hard-boiled dialogue Raymond Chandler wrote for the screenplay of *Double Indemnity* developed as a joke – a way of circumventing the limits on language and behaviour imposed by the highly restrictive Hays Code. Kael argued, in an essay written in 1981, that as soon as the Code lost its influence and explicit sexual dialogue began to be heard in movies, the 'terse, racy metaphors' exchanged by Bogart and Bacall, Stanwyck and MacMurray, lost their point and dwindled away; rightly so, she suggested, since they were 'ludicrous in a contemporary film with four-letter words and naked lovers'. Kael's reaction, when the director Lawrence Kasdan included exactly this type of sexual sparring match in his first feature film *Body Heat* – a remake of *Double Indemnity* set in Florida – was ridicule. Kasdan 'has modern characters talking as if they'd been boning up on Chandler novels', she mocked, 'and he doesn't know whether he wants laughs or not'. This was Kael missing the point on a grand scale, as though the underlying themes of *film noir* – and their oblique but vital relation to language – were as opaque to her as the dark interiors and atmospheric lighting which were (and continue to be) its visual trademark. There is far more to films like *Double Indemnity* and *Body Heat* than sexual banter, an uneasy sense of menace and the presence of a beautiful, homicidal woman who dupes men into committing murder for her; more than any other Hollywood genre, it has startling things to say about relationships between men and women, providing an adversarial reading of female sexuality which many film-goers find as compelling – perhaps more so – at the end of the twentieth century as they did in the 1940s. Indeed, if *Double Indemnity* can be read at some level as a joke, the same cannot be said of its linear descendant, John Dahl's *The Last Seduction* (1993). This stark, shocking thriller could with some justification claim to be the most *noir* film ever to come out of Hollywood, yet the fears and anxieties it addresses are not a million miles distant from those bubbling under the murder and double-cross plot in Wilder's classic movie.

What these might be is hinted at in a key scene towards the end of *Double Indemnity*, when MacMurray and Stanwyck confront each other at the Glendale house where they first met. Stanwyck's husband is dead, strangled by MacMurray, who subsequently faked his fall from a train to claim his insurance money, but the lovers no longer trust each other; believing Stanwyck to be unfaithful, MacMurray has already transferred his affections to her stepdaughter, hypocritically comforting the girl as she grieves for the father whose death is – or should be – on his conscience. When he finally challenges Stanwyck, she produces a gun and shoots him in the arm. Clearly intending to finish him off, she raises the gun to fire again but is unable to pull the trigger. 'Why don't you shoot again, baby?' MacMurray taunts her. 'Don't tell me it's because you've been in love with me all this time.'

Stanwyck pauses, her face softening and becoming more expressive. 'No, I never loved you, Walter. Not you or anybody else. I'm rotten to the heart. I used you just as you said. That's all you ever meant to me . . . until a minute ago when I couldn't fire that second shot. I never thought that could happen to me.' MacMurray's response is contemptuous, framed in terms that suggest he has belatedly recognised the commercial nature of the bargain he made with Stanwyck: 'Sorry, baby, I'm not buying.'

'I'm not asking you to buy,' she says wonderingly. 'Just hold me close.' MacMurray takes her in his arms, the camera lingering on Stanwyck's face as it becomes tender, vulnerable, dreamy. Her reverie is broken by a spasm of alarm whose cause is revealed to the audience a split second later as MacMurray, still embracing her, fires the gun he has taken from her and kills her.

In these dramatic moments, several themes are laid bare: the coldness underlying the sexual promise of the *femme fatale*, the inevitability of the fate facing the man who gets involved with her, the spark of decency which she is unable to quench in him (and which leads the wounded MacMurray to effect a reconciliation between Stanwyck's stepdaughter and her estranged boyfriend). Yet the real mystery of the film resides in Stanwyck's brief moment of repentance – of transfiguration almost, as the lighting implies – and whether or not it is genuine. MacMurray shoots her anyway but a doubt remains: has she been destroyed by his anger or by his inability, now as at the beginning of the film, to discern her true feelings?

What is being addressed here, however inarticulately, is the enigma not just of female sexuality but of femininity itself. Can a man ever trust a woman, even when she is pleading for her life? What goes through Stanwyck's mind in those last few seconds when she cannot fire the gun? It is important to remember that the whole story is narrated by MacMurray in the form of a taped confession; although we see Stanwyck directly, through the camera's lens, we are constantly nudged into reacting in a certain way by MacMurray's voice-over. Even more to the point, the confession is directed at Edward G. Robinson, an insurance claims investigator with a seriously jaundiced view of women. (He narrowly escaped marriage, he tells MacMurray in an earlier discussion about women, when he discovered that his prospective bride was not only a bigamist but *dyed her hair*.) In the film's final scene, as MacMurray lies weakened by loss of blood from the wound in his arm, the tough-talking Robinson provides absolution of a sort by offering him a light – reversing a visual trope in which MacMurray has always been on hand to light Robinson's cigarettes – as though he realises his own good fortune in not being taken in. *There but for the grace of God* is the father figure's clear message as they wait for the police to arrive.

In films like *Double Indemnity* and more recent Hollywood scenarios revolving around a *femme fatale* such as *Fatal Attraction*, there is an inherent and unresolved confusion. Ostensibly we are being warned about the danger to men represented by the sexually uninhibited female, yet who, in the final analysis, is she *fatale* to? Barbara Stanwyck and Glenn Close come to sticky ends; in both films, the penalty for being a successful seductress is death. It isn't clear whether the retributive ending of Billy Wilder's *Double Indemnity* was dictated by the Hays Code, but it's instructive to compare it with what happens in James M. Cain's original novella. In this version the insurance company for which Walter works, seeking to avoid a scandal, connives at his escape by boat to South America, where a familiar figure joins him on deck – Phyllis, his partner in crime, whom he now knows to be a serial killer with half a dozen victims to her credit. (She has, it turns out, despatched her husband's first wife and several other unfortunate patients for whom she worked as a private nurse.)

'We could be married, Walter,' this vision from hell murmurs, and the two of them stare out to sea for a very long time. Then, reinstating the mythic element which is completely absent from the film, there comes a chilling exchange. Phyllis remarks enigmatically that 'the time has come', and when Walter asks what she means she replies calmly: 'For me to meet my bridegroom. The only one I ever loved. One night I'll drop off the stern of the ship. Then, little by little I'll feel his icy fingers creeping into my heart.' Her fate, in contrast to the movie, is self-imposed, even sought: leaping from the ship into the moonlit water where the dark outline of a basking shark is already visible. The novella ends with Walter preparing to go with her, tagging along like a little dog who cannot do anything but follow where his mistress leads – even in the knowledge that the blood seeping from his wounded arm will inevitably attract the hungry predator.

What we have here is a much more chilling exegesis of male–female relations than in the film, one in which a woman's sexuality is characterised as aiming beyond her present lover – beyond a series of husbands and lovers – towards someone or something that exists only in the symbolic order. In the 1940s and 1950s, when both the production code and conventional morality limited the way in which this subject could be explored, it surfaced on screen in nuances and in scenarios which, like the famous shoot-out in a hall of mirrors in Orson Welles's *The Lady from Shanghai* (1948), hinted that the real theme was anxiety about female sexual identity. By 1971, when Alan J. Pakula came to make *Klute*, the stylish *film noir* which won Jane Fonda an Oscar for her role as the actress/call girl Bree Daniels, this element had become more explicit. The film is ostensibly about a cop's search for a missing engineer, a family man from Pennsylvania whose disappearance in New York has baffled the FBI; the only clue is a series of obscene letters written to Fonda/Daniels. The engineer is a cipher and the incorruptible cop, played by Donald Sutherland, hardly a fully developed character. The focus of the film is Bree Daniels, whose interactions with clients, directors, model agency bosses and her psychoanalyst are exposed to the viewer in a compelling cinematic exercise.

Is she acting? Which is her real self? These are questions Bree cannot answer, her responses varying at different points in the film. 'You don't have to care about anybody,' she says, explaining to her analyst why she enjoys being a prostitute. 'You don't have to like anybody. You just lead them by the ring in their nose in the direction you think they want to go in.' When she begins an affair with the investigator, John Klute, she is reduced to incoherence: 'My body feels . . . I enjoy . . . uh, making love with him . . . which is a baffling and bewildering experience for me. I've never felt this before.'

The film is a voyeur's paradise, in which a series of men – an elderly client, Klute himself, the killer – keep Bree under surveillance. Its climax takes place in a garment factory where rows of women's dresses hang on rails like ghostly presences, emphasising the central role in the film of female identity. Bree has gone there to seek help from its owner, the client for whom she performs a celebrated striptease earlier in the movie, slowly stripping off a shimmering silver sheath dress while describing her supposed fantasy about an older man; the mercantile nature of their bargain is revealed (again) by the fact that he has fled his office, leaving her an envelope containing money when what she needs is sanctuary from a killer. Cornered by the murderer in the empty factory, Bree is forced to listen to a tape in which he tortures and murders one of her friends, a fate which is clearly also intended for her until she is rescued at the last minute by John Klute.

The implication of the scene, that sexual role-playing has fatal consequences for women, drives Bree from New York but not into any more definite form of resolution, such as a permanent relationship with Klute. In the final moments of the film, as they leave her empty apartment to go their separate ways, she observes in a puzzled tone: 'It's hard for me to say it. I'm going to miss him.' Yet the bleak truth about her sexuality has already been revealed in an earlier conversation with her analyst. In a faint echo of Phyllis's declaration at the end of *Double Indemnity* (the novella, not the film), Bree admits: 'What I would really like is to be faceless and bodiless and left alone.'

Klute is a milestone in *film noir* because it is a lot more frank about its subject-matter than its antecedents. The supposed mystery – the search for the missing engineer – is merely a frame for the real inquiry, which is about the mask-like nature of female sexuality. If a woman cannot even know herself, how is a man ever to get a hold on her? Yet the presence of another, submerged, anxiety is suggested by the film's title, which shies away from admitting its real focus – the woman – and reasserts instead the significance of a man. There is a theme here which still cannot be acknowledged openly, something to do with the male characters and their role; what that might be becomes clearer in a film made a decade later, Kasdan's misunderstood (by Pauline Kael at least) and underrated *Body Heat* (1981). In this strikingly erotic thriller, the director paired Kathleen Turner with William Hurt, whose reprise of the MacMurray role in *Double Indemnity* had him playing not an insurance salesman but a vain and incompetent lawyer – an archetype, in fact, of the dumb blond who is a striking feature of these later, more knowing examples of *film noir*.

We first see Ned Racine (Hurt) in court, making a complete mess of a case involving – of all things – municipal toilets and being ticked off for his ineptitude by the judge. Soon he encounters Turner, giving an uncharacteristic performance as Maddy Walker, a hyperventilating bored wife and sex bomb. 'My temperature runs a couple of degrees higher, around a hundred,' she smoulders to Hurt at one steamy moment. Her contempt for him is unconcealed, consisting of jibes like 'You're not too smart, are you? I like that in a man' and 'Does chat like this work with most women?' Hurt takes these remarks not as the truth but as a challenge, allowing himself to be drawn into a classic *noir* plot to murder Turner's rich husband, played by William Crenna. Distracted by narcissistic illusions about his sexual performance, Hurt is so busy preening and strutting that it takes him most of the film to realise, several steps behind the audience, that Turner has chosen him not for his prowess in bed but for his track record of making a mess of past cases.

What distinguishes the film from Wilder's *Double Indemnity*, apart from the explicit sex scenes, is the ending. Turner dies, apparently, in an explosion in a summer house and Hurt winds up in jail, accused of murdering her husband. In the last few minutes, however, it finally dawns on him that Turner is still alive – that she has assumed another woman's identity in a meticulously planned operation. The movie ends with a confirmatory shot of Turner on a faraway beach, enjoying the fruits of her wicked machinations, a denouement prefigured, for those alert enough to catch it, by a clever trick at the film's climactic moment, just before the explosion. Hurt has gone to the summer house on Turner's orders to retrieve the victim's glasses, supposedly left there by a blackmailer, but even he has begun to wonder why she cannot get them back herself. Suspecting a trap, he dithers until Turner appears and demands to know whether he has been inside, giving him a lingering, reproachful glance before heading towards the summer house herself. Suddenly she turns to face him: 'Ned, no matter what you think, I do love you.' Then, before she has quite reached the door of the summer house, she literally vanishes from the screen.

It's a brief but symbolic moment, easy to overlook but a stunning visual representation of the idea that women are protean creatures, able to transmute their forms and elude men altogether. This theme, and the parallel one of a bumbling male incompetence which makes them easy targets for clever, unscrupulous women, is given full rein in John Dahl's 1993 thriller *The Last Seduction*. Linda Fiorentino, whose role in the film has justly been described as that of *Uber*-bitch, dupes not one but two dumb blonds – her husband Clay, played by Bill Pullman, and her lover Mike (Peter Berg).

The plot is complex, beginning with Pullman and Fiorentino pulling off a million-dollar drug deal in New York. Pullman very nearly makes a mess of it and, under extreme stress, strikes Fiorentino across the face. This slap is Fiorentino's apparent motive for taking off with the loot and hiding under an assumed name in a provincial town in upstate New York where she immediately picks up Berg in a bar. Berg's complicity, first in her sexual games and then in a preposterous murder plot involving the insurance company for which they both work, is based explicitly on the notion that Fiorentino can restore his damaged self-esteem, still smarting from a disastrous off-screen marriage in Buffalo. When a friend asks what he sees in Fiorentino, he replies candidly: 'Maybe a new set of balls.'

Fiorentino makes even less of an attempt than previous *femmes fatales* to hide her true nature, telling Berg she comes from 'a galaxy far far away' and announcing that she's a bitch – a 'total fucking bitch' in fact, which, since they're having sex at the time, Berg takes to be a pun. Fooling himself that they are going to set up house together in New York, Berg agrees to murder a total stranger for a cut of his insurance money – and belatedly discovers that the trussed-up victim in a Manhattan apartment is not the wife-beater he has been led to believe but Fiorentino's enraged husband. In a scene of chilling manipulation, Fiorentino enters the room where the two men have just come to a shocked mutual realisation of her treachery and kills Pullman herself. Then she goads Berg into raping her noisily, and on tape, as she gasps down the phone line for help from the emergency operator.

It is at this point, just before Berg is arrested, that we discover what Fiorentino has known from some time – that Berg is such a sexual ingenue that his 'wife' in Buffalo was actually a male transvestite. 'You married a man, you farm faggot,' Fiorentino taunts, plunging us precipitously into the heart of the male anxiety which drives *film noir*: not just that women are unknowable, but that men are such slavish sexual idiots that they can be duped even by the simulacrum of a woman.

Berg, like William Hurt in *Body Heat*, winds up in prison, desperately trying to persuade his lawyer of his innocence. The attorney is unconvinced by Berg's tangled and improbable explanation of events, warning him that if he cannot come up with a better story, he is facing the electric chair. 'There may be one thing,' Berg says suddenly, brightening up, and at that moment the camera cuts to the rainy exterior of Fiorentino's apartment block in New York. She leaves the building in a slinky ankle-length dress, shielded by a diminutive manservant holding an umbrella, and settles down in the back of a stretch limo. Removing her dark glasses, she takes out a lighter and burns the piece of evidence on which Berg's life depends, raising her arm languorously above her head as the car rounds the corner into Broadway.

Unlike Stanwyck, she isn't punished; unlike MacMurray, there's no father figure to absolve the poor sucker who is left to carry the can. Indeed, Berg's boasting at the beginning of the film – 'I'm hung like a horse' – is exposed as a pathetic sham. Fiorentino's predatory sexuality has achieved its aim, which is not to take lover after lover but to be altogether free of men. Still stunningly sexy, her dress split to the thigh, at the end of the film she simply goes off with the cash, leaving a trail of dead and emasculated men in her wake.

The French psychoanalyst Jacques Lacan once remarked, somewhat gnomically, that the partner of a woman is solitude. It is a formula which might, at first sight, be interpreted as a denial of female sexuality, a suggestion that celibacy is simultaneously women's goal and true estate. In the context of *film noir*, however, it could equally be read as an expression of quite the opposite sentiment, which is to say an anxious recognition of women's sexual *autonomy*. There is nothing asexual or nun-like about Kathleen Turner or Linda Fiorentino as they bask in the enjoyment of their ill-gotten gains; on the contrary, the female stars of these films exploit heterosexual male narcissism and its dependence on female affirmation to achieve a state of erotic *in*dependence. No longer wives or mistresses, certainly not mothers – the ineffectualness of the men is underlined by the fact that not one of them, whether husband or lover, succeeds in getting his inamorata pregnant – their condition at the end of both neo-*noir* movies amounts to a visual display of female auto-eroticism which chillingly confirms the notion of male redundancy. At a moment in history when the power relation between men and women is both fluid and, in some quarters, bitterly contested, the continuing success of *film noir* is a testament to the pleasure people take in having their worst fears confirmed – at least at the safe level of fantasy. Whatever its relation to real life, and I suspect that men and women enjoy it for very different reasons, its stark message for the final decade of the twentieth century can now be spelled out. Men are weak. And the lady always vanishes.

Single, White, Fertile

IT MUST HAVE been one of the most unflattering pictures ever taken of a normally glamorous woman: Paula Yates arriving at Heathrow Airport from Australia, weary lines creasing her eyes and mouth, dark roots visible in her dyed blonde hair, lips smeared with salmon-pink lipstick as though she'd hastily applied it on the plane. 'Paula: I'll fight to keep my children' was the accompanying headline in the *Evening Standard*, above a story announcing that drugs – allegedly a small quantity of opium – had been found at Yates's Chelsea home during her absence on the other side of the world. It didn't help that she was wearing a wildly inappropriate black cocktail dress with a plunging neckline, giving her the appearance of someone emerging bleary-eyed from a nightclub at dawn rather than a defiant mother battling for custody of her children. Nor did the fact that, as the *Evening Standard* revealed, she had flown to London without her sick two-month-old daughter Heavenly Hiraani Tiger Lily, who was being cared for by her father, the rock star Michael Hutchence, in Australia. The subtext was blatant: Yates's predicament was hardly surprising when she looked such a mess *and* had abandoned her baby in order to make her hasty trip to London. Just to make things worse, an unfortunate coincidence of timing meant that Yates made her appearance on the front page of the *Standard* on the same day as Mandy Allwood, whose doctors were desperately trying to prevent her multiple pregnancy from miscarrying. The contest was straightforward, good mother versus bad, with no prizes for guessing who was the winner.

Ever since her divorce from Bob Geldof, Yates has been a figure of fun, ridiculed for giving her children silly names, for having her breasts enlarged, and for dashing off a self-serving autobiography in an indecently short time. Ian Hislop, editor of *Private Eye*, mauled her mercilessly when she was ill-advised enough to appear on the satirical TV programme *Have I Got News For You*, mocking her writing, her vocabulary and her breasts with equal ferocity. The stories which appeared after the alleged drugs find, however, broke new ground. Yates was portrayed as a careless mother, a divorcee with a younger lover who had exposed her daughters to drugs – thus pushing one of the late twentieth century's most effective panic buttons – and then compounded the offence by leaving her tiny baby on another continent while she flew home to face the music. And what was the sequel to these dramatic events? Yates's recently appointed PR woman resigned in a fit of righteous indignation – a loss most of us could bear with equanimity – but that was all. No charges were brought against Yates, Hutchence or anyone else who lived in her house, while her childcare arrangements continued much as before.

Paula Yates may be a silly, vain woman, but there is no evidence that she neglects or in any other way mistreats her daughters. On the contrary, she has written two books about childcare which irritated many readers with their noisy advocacy of a very traditional model of motherhood, including an insistence that women with small children should stay at home – advice she herself ignored when she was a presenter on *The Big Breakfast*. And while some of the most mawkish paragraphs in her autobiography are about her daughters, there is a transparent sincerity to her protestations that 'I've always tried to do my best for all of my . . . children and they, in turn, have given my life a real focus. They were, and still are, absolutely central to my existence.' It was simply Yates's bad luck that, for a moment at least, she appeared to embody everything that's considered bad about mothering at a time when the collapse of the nuclear family, and the consequent rise in the number of single-parent families, has produced a fevered debate about the way children are brought up. Single mothers, a category so elastic that it can be stretched to accommodate any woman who isn't living with her husband and two perfect children in a state of familial bliss, are currently being blamed for everything from truancy to exam failure to murder, and Yates was a pathetically easy target. Divorced from Geldof after an acrimonious separation, enjoying herself with a younger lover whom she injudiciously described in her autobiography as a 'sexy love god', her name connected however tangentially with a drugs bust: for the purposes of tabloid newspapers like the *Daily Mirror* it was an open-and-shut case. Yet the only charge that could be made to stick against Yates was that she had given her children outlandish names – Fifi Trixiebelle, Peaches and Pixie as well as Heavenly Hiraani – and it must have been apparent to the densest reader that this does not rate very high in the contemporary catalogue of child abuse; she had not beaten, starved or sexually abused them, and all four girls had fathers who appeared content, to put it no higher, with their children's unusual nomenclature. Indeed, the irony was that Yates, with her old-fashioned ideas about raising children and a wife's role in marriage, would probably have *agreed* with the sentiments of many of her detractors. How many women in their thirties would admit, as she did in her autobiography, that the greatest social revolution of the century had completely passed them by? 'Bob said it was demeaning for women to be supported by men,' she wrote about the period immediately following her marriage to Geldof, in a tone of genuine incomprehension. 'This was a new concept for me.'

The pillorying of Paula Yates in the press has to be seen in a context in which mother-bashing headlines are an almost daily occurrence. 'Pregnant at 15, married at 16, and divorcing at 17', was how the *Daily Mail* announced a typical front-page assault on single mothers, adding for good measure: 'Just what does this girl's story tell us about morality in Britain today?' The *Sunday Telegraph*, which has a similar agenda, did not actually name single and/or working mothers when it led its front page with the startling contention that 'Four out of ten children [are] "mentally ill"' but the story which followed was in no doubt who was to blame:

Up to 40 per cent of the nation's children have mental health disorders including psychosis, eating problems and suicidal tendencies, according to evidence submitted to MPs.
Leading psychologists say that the breakdown of the family

has created a new generation of 'latchkey children' – many of whom suffer neglect and abuse.

Who is responsible for creating 'latchkey children'? Since fathers have never been expected to be at home when their children return from school, the answer is obvious. The story marked a return to a favourite theme for the *Sunday Telegraph*, which had run a leader page piece entreating 'Spare the job, mother, and save the child' only four weeks earlier. The article was uncompromising, as even the byline announced: 'The chief cause of juvenile delinquency is the working mother, says Lynette Burrows.' Writing about the campaign to 'remoralise our youth' in the wake of 'several horrible murders' – presumably she was thinking about, among others, the killing of two-year-old James Bulger in Liverpool by two ten-year-old boys and the murder by a teenage boy of the London head teacher Philip Lawrence – Burrows wrote despairingly about 'young tearaways' who observe only 'the law of the jungle'. She savaged laws which supposedly outlaw smacking and fiscal policies which discriminate against women who stay at home with their children, but reserved her strongest criticism for the effect which jobs have on mothers:

> Capitalism is devouring the family and the effect is pernicious. One reason why today's unrealistic approach to childrearing has taken hold is that women have been collectivised and demoralised. Millions of women who were once mistresses in their own homes have become mere paid servants in the businesses of others. Even though they were only the boss in something as small as a family, it was the most important thing in their lives, and it gave them confidence and authority. They knew about bringing up children and would have been affronted by today's suggestion that they needed lessons in doing it.

Referring to the widely publicised campaign on moral issues launched by Philip Lawrence's widow, Frances, Burrows argued that such initiatives could not succeed unless 'mothers take them up in their own homes and neighbourhoods. And they cannot do that unless they are there in more than a part-time capacity.' Women, she insisted, 'are largely responsible for how young people turn out. Men traditionally have rightly [*sic*] deferred to women in training the young, but today's women are ill-equipped to do it.' These are breath-taking arguments from a stridently right-wing newspaper whose editorial line would normally offer uncritical support to a free market in labour, as well as insisting on the pivotal role of a male-dominated organisation – the Church of England – in setting moral standards. An atmosphere of moral panic is not, however, conducive to consistency, and it is no accident that the anguished and emotional debate about the behaviour of children and adolescents is taking place at a moment when many people are suffering from not just *fin de siècle* but millennarian anxiety. Yet the oddest thing about Burrows's article is not its quasi-Marxist denunciation of the alienation of women in the contemporary workforce. It is the complete absence of the word 'father' from her analysis – a feature her article shares with many others on this theme, even in newspapers with a more liberal agenda, such as the *Guardian*. It is a strange fact that when the collapse of the nuclear family is under discussion, the spotlight falls not on the *couples* who are supposed to be its bedrock but exclusively on the female partner.

Think for a moment: have you ever seen a headline announcing that 'working dads are blamed for children's failures'? That headline appeared, with one significant difference, on the front page of the *Guardian* in February 1997; it was of course working *mums*, not dads, whose influence on children was under attack. The *Guardian* story was a trail for a *Panorama* programme on BBC television the same evening which claimed to have discovered 'middle-class deprivation' among families where *both* parents chose to work full-time. The entire programme was devoted to the findings of a single academic study of 600 families in Barking and Dagenham, which suggested that children whose mothers worked full-time were twice as likely to fail their GCSEs as those with mothers working part-time. The media got so excited about this one limited study that the *Sunday Times* reported it on its front page the day before the programme was transmitted under the uncompromising headline 'Children of working mothers face exam failure'. Alternative explanations of the findings, such as the question of whether the parents in the study were able to afford decent childcare, were not canvassed in any of the frankly sensational front-page coverage.

Meanwhile, as the backwash from the *Panorama* programme continued to fill the comment pages, the contrary opinion of a leading paediatrician, Dr Ian Roberts, director of the Child Monitoring Unit at the Institute of Child Health in London, was relegated to page 10 of the *Daily Telegraph*. Dr Roberts pointed out that an examination by his institute of *eight* international research studies showed that small children who are put into day care have higher intelligence scores than pre-school infants who stay at home. Dr Roberts insisted:

> There isn't a scrap of evidence that putting children in day care while their mothers go to work is bad for their health or education. On the contrary, the evidence from well-conducted trials suggests that it's very good for children.

This view was supported by another expert in the field – John Ermisch, professor of economics at Essex University, who told the following weekend's *Observer* that most recent statistics indicated that children with two working parents performed better at school. Ermisch's claim was based on the largest study of working mothers undertaken in the 1990s, and involved examining the effect of family background on the educational results of 5,500 households and nearly 1,600 pupils over five years. (It also emerged that the *Panorama* programme had been fiercely criticised within the BBC itself at the organisation's weekly programme review board.) This is what Ermisch told the *Observer*:

> There is no evidence that having a mother in employment when the child was aged 14 reduces educational attainment, and it may indeed increase the odds that the child obtains qualifications of A-level or higher. Having a mother in a managerial job when a boy was aged 14 significantly increases his educational attainment.

Although the *Daily Telegraph* gave some space – around six column inches – to Dr Roberts's rebuttal of the *Panorama* programme, it attached much greater weight to the views of its resident columnist, Janet Daley. She got a banner headline for her argument that 'a really selfless mother won't work full-time'. Daley found herself in a slightly awkward position as a woman who had always worked, even when her children were young, but she salvaged what she could from this contradiction by making a distinction between full- and part-time jobs:

I have been a working woman all my life, but I never worked full-time when my children were young. Even with a half-time career, I learnt rather a lot about substitute child-care. However kind, well trained and intelligent the people are who look after your children, unless they raise them from birth through to university entrance, they will never know and respond to them the way that their own mother can. Nor will they have the long-term interest in the children's future that makes a parent's attention so unique – whether it involves supervising a 10-year-old's homework or listening to the anxious confidences of an adolescent.

What's interesting here is how the ground has shifted, even for right-wing newspapers like the *Telegraph*; the argument is no longer polarised around working mothers versus stay-at-home mothers but focuses on the *amount* of time mothers spend at work – reflecting, almost certainly, the number of women with children on the editorial staff of most newspapers. But the most revealing section of Daley's article was her peroration. Fearlessly laying into mothers who, unlike her, work full-time when their children are small, Daley thundered:

I will say this straight out and then wait for the tide of scathing abuse: being a good mother – or, to put it less judgementally, the kind of mother who produces successful, confident children – requires a degree of selflessness. Even – dare I breathe the words – an element of self-sacrifice.

This self-denial need only be temporary – protecting the most crucial years of child-rearing or even the most critical hours of the day – but it is the willingness of the woman to contemplate such sacrifice that is significant.

Of course it is unfair. Small children are self-centred and demanding, but that is because their needs are so very urgent. What I suspect is damaging the motivation of the failing children in the *Panorama* research is not just the loss of maternal attention, but the sense that they are not the absolute centre of their mothers' lives: being fitted in around the edges, however fondly, is just not the same.

There could hardly be a more blatant example of the wildly differing standards by which men and women are judged. When *men* go out to work, leaving their children in someone else's hands, it's because they are doing the serious job of bread-winning. Some of them – the Duke of York is an obvious example, his career in the Navy requiring long periods at sea – barely see their children from one month to the next. Indeed, we are often asked to sympathise with men for the long hours they have to work, especially in Britain where the Major government fought tooth and nail against attempts by the EC to impose quite modest limits on the working week. Work, for men, is an arduous and often unrewarding activity undertaken for the higher good of providing for the women and children at home. Clearly this is far from the whole picture and depends on variables like class, pay and occupation, but the salient point is that I have never heard the accusation of selfishness levelled at men who work full-time. When *women* with children take full-time jobs, however, the meaning of going out to work abruptly changes. Even though they earn less than men – the Central Statistical Office observed in 1995 that 'there is a larger proportion of women at the lower end of the pay range than men' – and are more likely to be found in low-status secretarial, clerical and menial jobs, we are supposed to believe that they enter the employment market for frivolous or even hedonistic reasons. (Maybe Daley should write a book on typical female occupations. *The Joy of Cleaning* perhaps?)

This is not to argue that women don't enjoy having jobs but

to suggest that their motives for working outside the home, and their feelings about what they do, are as varied as those of men. (Some of them, for example, just need the money.) The good news, though, about articles like Daley's is that while they attempt to set out a straightforward moral agenda, they are actually symptomatic of the muddle which not just conservative newspapers but the mainstream political parties have got into on this subject. A couple of days after the *Panorama* programme was transmitted on prime-time television, the following headline appeared on page 2 of the *Guardian*: 'Jobs drive for lone parents'. The paper reported a government initiative to spend £20 million 'to help move 100,000 single parents from welfare into work', a scheme announced by the right-wing social security secretary, Peter Lilley. Nowhere in the article about Lilley's new Parent Plus initiative was there a suggestion that this might be a bad thing, in spite of the attacks on working mothers which had been going on all week; hilariously, given that Lilley had in the past won ovations from Conservative party conferences for his rabble-rousing denunciations of single mothers, the minister had suddenly chosen to present himself in the guise of the single parents' friend. Taking a rather different tone from the one he adopted in 1992 when he claimed to have 'a little list . . . of young ladies' who got pregnant outside marriage in order to get state benefits, Lilley insisted:

Most lone parents want to work but this group need particular help to break out of the benefit trap. It is important that children grow up seeing parents as breadwinners and not the state as sole provider.

The Conservative government's initiative was a belated response to a speech the previous month by the Labour leader, Tony Blair, in which he promised to introduce a range of measures to help lone parents return to work. As a self-declared Christian socialist who believes in 'family values', Blair is in a difficult position. 'Children raised by two parents in a stable, loving relationship *do* get a head start,' he wrote in an essay entitled 'Valuing Families' in 1995, but he heads a party whose radical wing does not share his enthusiasm for the nuclear family (or, indeed, for the old-fashioned heterosexual unions which were its foundation). In fact, it seems likely that politicians of *both* main political parties are motivated as much by financial motives as by a desire to help single parents; regardless of ideology, the cost of state benefits to support them and their families is currently running at around £8 *billion* a year, a dauntingly large portion of government expenditure. What's curious, though, is the way in which Lilley used the studiedly gender-neutral term 'lone parents' when the people he had in mind were overwhelmingly female. The government's own statistics show that in 1992–3, 18 per cent of dependent children lived in a lone-mother family and only 2 per cent with a lone father; another way of expressing this figure is that single mothers outnumber lone fathers by *nine to one*. At the same time, the proportion of families headed by a single mother is rising dramatically: from 7 to 20 per cent between 1971 and the early 1990s. This is bad news for British governments of any political persuasion, cash-strapped as they are likely to be for the foreseeable future, and it creates the following bind: much as politicians revere the ideal of the traditional family, with father going out to work and a stable home presided over by a fulfilled, non-working mother, the reality is that more and more children are being raised by single mothers whose poverty places a heavy burden on the state. What to do about this is a conundrum which produces conflicting policies and announcements, depending on which aspect of the problem is causing popular outrage – failures of parenting or the burden on the Exchequer – at any given moment. Right-wing dogma prefers mothers not to work at all but is, if anything, even more reluctant to bear the cost of supporting their families; the choices, therefore, are to get them off welfare by encouraging them to work – which involves addressing the question of who will provide and pay for childcare – or to face an uncomfortable truth about why single-parent families are so poor in the first place. And that requires, once again, getting to grips with the F-word.

Absent fathers: that, in a nutshell, is the problem John Major's government was trying to address when it set up the much-maligned Child Support Agency. The organisation's aim, as stated in its annual report, is 'to replace a child maintenance system which was failing large numbers of children, the parents with whom they lived and the general taxpayer'; its principal task, laid down in the Child Support Acts of 1991 and 1995, is 'to ensure that parents who live apart meet their financial responsibility to their children whenever they can afford to do so'. The scale of this task is indicated by a single statistic, the CSA's live caseload in 1997, which was 1.8 million cases.

The CSA's inefficiency when it was first set up, and a few well-publicised instances in which men received huge bills which turned out to be inaccurate, have tended to overshadow its achievements. Yet, now that all the fuss has died down and teething problems have been ironed out, it is possible to examine its statistics and get a sense of the extraordinary state of affairs it was set up to deal with. Since 1995, no absent parent has been required to pay more than 30 per cent of net income in child support; indeed, far from facing bills running into hundreds of pounds, the *average* amount due under a CSA assessment is around £25 per week. Even so, the CSA has had to cope not only with the problem of separated couples where one partner is reluctant to co-operate with its financial investigations but with parents who have vanished altogether. In 1995-6 alone it undertook more than 55,000 specialist traces in order to track down missing parents, bringing the total since its inception to nearly 133,000. We are talking here, not to put too fine a point on it, about parents who have disappeared without a forwarding address, leaving their partners and offspring to get by as best they can – either by working, existing on handouts from their families or claiming state benefits. And what kind of people might these be? Here is the only clue we get from the CSA annual report:

> In many of these cases our staff have to *establish paternity* [my italics], which can be a difficult and sensitive process, requiring interviewing of alleged absent parents, DNA testing and court proceedings. We have introduced improved guidelines to support staff involved in tracing absent parents.

In other words, CSA staff are having to confront *fathers* who have not only abandoned their families but deny all responsibility for them. In fact, according to the agency's press office, 95.2 per cent of the people who have to make regular payments are absent fathers, and only 4.8 per cent absent mothers. Here is another fascinating statistic from the agency's annual report: since the introduction of a DNA Paternity Testing Scheme in 1995, 85 per cent of those tested have 'proved to be the parent'. Once again, if we put this into plain English, it means that of those men who protest, when confronted by a CSA official, that they never met the woman in question or merely bought her a drink at a disco, seventeen out of twenty are lying. And what they are trying to avoid is paying around £25 a week for the upkeep of the children they have fathered.

In a rational world, these figures might well indicate some sort of crisis about how we as a society bring up and support children. But is it really a crisis, as everyone from newspaper columnists and documentary-makers to politicians keeps telling us, of *motherhood*? It would not to be difficult to mount an alternative case in which it is *mothers*, whether they stay at home or work part-time or have full-time jobs, who are struggling to maintain some semblance of family life in the face of a wholesale flight by *men* from their responsibilities. Organisations like the lobbying group Families Need Fathers counter this charge by claiming that many men are unwillingly ejected from their families by women who find new partners or simply prefer to be on their own, an argument which fails to address the crucial question of what kind of fathering they were providing before the relationship broke down; choosing to be a single mother is such a momentous decision for most women that they are unlikely to make it without good reasons, which might include a partner's violence, infidelity or a disinclination to accept his share of parental responsibility. Are we really to believe that of those hundred thousand or so fathers whose whereabouts were unknown, until the CSA tracked them down at the taxpayer's expense, every single one of them was unreasonably thrown out by his wife or partner?

There is a well-known psychological mechanism, called displacement, which transfers anxiety from one subject which is too painful to contemplate on to another, easier target. The most obvious explanation for the sometimes daily attacks on mothers in the British press, whether they appear in a newspaper such as the *Telegraph* or the supposedly more liberal *Guardian*, is that we live in a moral climate which would rather scapegoat women than face unpalatable truths about men. Perhaps it is *men* who should be spending more time with their children, and be more involved in their day-to-day care, and more realistic about the cost of bringing up a child from the day it is born to the moment it leaves school or university – but that would involve a wholesale reappraisal of the way we approach the different demands of work and of being a parent. It would also require a recognition of the extent to which we like the *idea* of children without being anything like so keen on the reality. Everyone loves imaginary babies, as evidenced by the speed with which an anti-abortion group raised tens of thousands of pounds in 1996 in the hope of persuading an anonymous pregnant woman in London not to abort one of the twins she was carrying. Yet the truth is that millions of real live children in Britain live below the poverty line – a fact which could just as easily be responsible for their failure to thrive educationally, morally or physically as the style of mothering they are receiving.

'One in three British babies born in poverty' was the headline above a front-page story in the *Independent on Sunday* as recently as November 1996; according to the accompanying text, the British government's own figures revealed that, in 1995–6, 215,000 babies were born into families which were receiving state benefits because they were on the breadline – 30 per cent of all the children born in that period. The figures, compiled by the House of Commons library from social security statistics, showed that more than 200,000 mothers received maternity payments from the social fund, and that 30,000 of these went to low-income families rather than people entirely dependent on state benefits. Using an entitlement to welfare benefits as an index of poverty, the paper also reported that the number of children living in families dependent on supplementary benefit had increased from one million in 1979, when the Conservatives returned to power, to 2.8 million on the roughly equivalent benefit, income support, in 1992.

Poverty, the growing inequality between rich and poor families, absent fathers, a state education system which fails thousands of poorer pupils: any or all of these could lie behind the crisis of unruly youth, if indeed there is one in Britain today rather than an unhealthy and sensational concentration on some high-profile cases. Why look for complex explanations, however, when that old standby, female altruism or its absence, is so easily to hand? What women have yet to learn is that as soon as they have a baby, they are unwittingly signing up to take part in a contest they can never win. In previous centuries mothers used to die for their offspring, either in childbirth or from complications afterwards, and those apparently self-immolating examples are still lodged, subliminally, in our brains. I say 'apparently' because puerperal fever and the other infections which carried women off were hardly a matter of choice, yet the pairing of motherhood and self-sacrifice is so firmly established that many people have never tried – wouldn't even want – to unpick it. In that sense, a mother can never be altruistic enough, for any decision which even has the appearance of putting her interests before those of her children – from taking a job or setting up with a new partner – merely emphasises how far she is from the ideal. Mothers are people who give something up, an assumption vividly expressed by the poet John Masefield when he wrote:

In the dark womb where I began
My mother's life made me a man.
Through all the months of human birth
Her beauty fed my common earth.
I cannot see, nor breathe, nor stir,
But through the death of some of her.

No one has ever written like this about *fathers*. The irony is that, while everything a woman does for her children is taken for granted, fathers are idealised and forgiven for their absences. Indeed, anyone who reads newspapers might come away with the impression that children who turn out well are a credit to their fathers, while those who go wrong, whether we are talking about teenagers failing their GCSEs or knifing their schoolmates, are the sole responsibility of their mothers. So deeply ingrained is this view that detectives hunting some particularly vicious rapist or serial killer more often than not announce that they are looking for a loner 'who lives with his mother' – and we all know what *that* means. Fathers are off the hook in this culture. Women, beware: never forget that all our hearts belong to Daddy.

The Love That Dare Not
Speak Its Name

IN THE SUMMER of 1994, a mystery which had tantalised the literary establishments of Paris, London and New York for forty years was abruptly and dramatically cleared up. Ever since its publication in 1954, controversy had raged around the sexually explicit novel *Histoire d'O*, not just because of its content but because no one could give a definitive answer to the question of whether its pseudonymous author, 'Pauline Réage', was a woman. Were these graphic scenes of women being raped, flogged and forced into prostitution really the product of a female imagination? Feminist critics in particular said not, arguing that the novel simply placed common male heterosexual fantasies in a female voice. Suddenly, though, the sceptics seemed to have been confounded. An article in the *New Yorker* confirmed that 'Réage' was in fact Dominique Aury, a critic and editor at the prestigious Gallimard publishing house.

Aury was not well known outside publishing circles, but her name had come up before in connection with *Histoire d'O*, making her one of the few women on whom suspicion had fallen. (Among the prime suspects, almost all of them men, only the names of André Malraux and Raymond Queneau would have been immediately recognisable outside France.) She had never previously admitted to writing the book, but this time, casting her previous reticence aside, she gave a lengthy interview to John de St Jorre, himself the author of a book about the Olympia Press which published the first English translation of O, in which she not only confirmed her authorship but provided a mass of detail about how, when and why she wrote it. Yet as fast as one mystery was cleared up, others emerged. First and most bizarrely, Dominique Aury turned out to be another pen-name, not quite invalidating the *New Yorker* scoop but blunting its impact with the admission that the creator of *O* was still clinging to a layer of disguise: 'She asked me not to publish [her real name], or the details of her surviving family, and this I agreed to,' St Jorre revealed. Then, by an eerie coincidence, no sooner had 'Dominique Aury' acquired a protective set of quotation marks than something similar happened to her first American translator. Towards the end of his long article, St Jorre suddenly suggested that the otherwise obscure Sabine d'Estrée – or 'Sabine d'Estrée' – was really a man, an American publisher named Richard Seaver.

St Jorre had, in effect, pulled off the double coup of solving a mystery and maintaining it at the same time. By the end of his account, while the reader undoubtedly knew a great deal more about the genesis of *O*, questions of identity and gender had not been entirely divorced from the heroine's slender and tormented form. The shadowy figure of a man lurked in the background, as translator if not author, as though the notion of *O* as the sole and unaided work of a woman was, even in the light of the 86-year-old Aury's admissions, not completely convincing. This is not as surprising as it sounds, for this is a case in which pre-existing ideas about the author's gender have undoubtedly coloured almost everything, favourable or otherwise, which has been written about the novel in the four decades since it appeared. An erotic or, depending on your taste, pornographic classic, *Histoire d'O* is unlike other celebrated examples of the genre – Cleland's *Fanny Hill*, for example – in that it has also, virtually from the moment of its first publication in French, enjoyed the additional cachet of intellectual respectability. Praised by Georges Bataille, within a year it had won a literary prize in France, the Prix Deux-Magots, whose previous winners included Queneau. In England, Graham Greene dubbed it 'a rare thing, a pornographic book well written and without a trace of obscenity', while J. G. Ballard hailed it as 'a deeply moral homily'. The London *Spectator* considered it 'a highly literary and imaginative work, the brilliance of whose style leaves one in no doubt whatever of the author's genius'. Many male critics, it is clear, simply loved the idea that a woman had written so erotically; in 1954, Anaïs Nin's pornographic sketches had not yet been collected and published, leaving 'Pauline Réage' the only woman in a hall of fame consisting of de Sade, Cleland, Joyce, Lawrence, Nabokov, Miller and Genet. Men thrilled to the notion that a woman had invented the story of O, a fashion photographer who voluntarily undergoes a sequence of sexual humiliations and beatings at the behest of her lover, René. *Histoire d'O* chronicles her descent into prostitution, into an acceptance of systematic floggings, even to the transfer of her 'ownership' from her lover René to a sinister (some might say risible) English aristocrat, Sir Stephen H. In a notorious passage, Sir Stephen arranges to have a ring inserted through her labia from which he suspends a tag bearing his name and insignia; an owl mask is placed over O's head and she is chained up, rendering her anonymous, dehumanised and universally available. 'Pauline Réage' supplied two endings to the novel, one of which is a promise of more of the same, while the other consists of two short sentences: 'Seeing herself about to be left by Sir Stephen, [O] preferred to die. To which he gave his consent.'

Most editions of *Histoire d'O*, however, conclude with an essay entitled 'A Slave's Revolt' by the distinguished writer and critic Jean Paulhan, a member of the Académie Française who worked with Aury at Gallimard. Insisting he did not know the true identity of 'Pauline Réage' – 'I don't even know who you are', he wrote unequivocally – Paulhan nevertheless used the essay to express his conviction that the author was a woman, citing as evidence all the little feminine details in the novel about dresses and underwear. What he really admired about the book, though, was its honesty:

Here we have it at last: a woman who admits it! Admits what? Exactly what women have always – and never more so than today – forbidden themselves to admit. Exactly what men have always accusingly said was true about them: that they never cease slavishly to obey their blood and temper; that, in them, everything, even their minds, even their souls, is dominated by their sex. That they have got incessantly to be fed, incessantly washed and burdened, incessantly beaten. That they have but one requirement, and that is simply of a good master who takes good care to keep his goodness in check and to be wary of it: for it will be to make themselves loved by others that they will put to use all the high-spiritedness, the joy, the gay disposition which becomes theirs as a result of our tenderness towards them when once we declare our tender feelings. That, in a word, one must have a whip in hand when one goes to visit them.

Most men, Paulhan hazarded, had dreamed of 'possessing' the Marquis de Sade's heroine, Justine. No woman, he added, had dreamed of *being* Justine – until 'Pauline Réage'. The novel, in other words, was important not just for its literary quality but for its unusual frankness in admitting to the innate masochism of female erotic fantasies.

Superficially at least, the revelations in the *New Yorker* appeared to support Paulhan's contention. Aury told John de St Jorre that the book was drawn from her own imagination, which appeared to leave little room for doubt: 'All I know is that they were honest fantasies – whether they were male or female, I couldn't say.' And yet, as in the matter of the real identity of 'Pauline Réage', things had no sooner been cleared up than they became more complicated. Aury revealed that she had written the novel as a gift for her then lover in an attempt to maintain his interest in her when their affair began to wane. Who was that lover? None other than the man who had written 'A Slave's Revolt', disclaiming all knowledge of the identity of the author of *Histoire d'O*. In other words that deception, in which Aury acquiesced, was the work of Jean Paulhan.

Here at last, emerging from a consciously constructed maze of concealed identities, is the man in the case. Aury was in her forties at the time she began to write the novel, Paulhan getting on for seventy and married to an invalid wife; in that sense, the fear that he might leave *her* represents a startling inversion of the power balance one might expect from their relative ages. Yet Aury was convinced that this older, glamorous man was on the verge of deserting her:

I wasn't young, I wasn't pretty, it was necessary to find other weapons. The physical side wasn't enough. The weapons, alas, were in the head. 'I'm sure you can't do that sort of thing,' he said. 'You think not?' I said. 'Well, I can try.'

The device worked. According to St Jorre, 'Paulhan loved it from the opening sentence and urged her on'. He described the novel, privately, as 'the most ardent love letter any man has ever received' and went on seeing Aury until his death in 1968.

What light does this shed on *Histoire d'O*? It is, to say the least, a startling revelation: a novel hailed for its courage in admitting that women secretly long to be dominated, that their most profound sexual response is to the biological imperative of submission, turns out to have been written out of a woman's fear of abandonment. The *New Yorker* article went on to reveal that Aury showed Paulhan the manuscript as it progressed and even read sections aloud to him, gauging his response and, it seems reasonable to assume, providing more of what he liked. So whose desire – and this is the absolutely central question – is being articulated in *Histoire d'O*?

It is worth recalling, at this point, that the true identity of its author is still unknown to the majority of the book's readers. She remains, to this day, Madame X writing as 'Dominique Aury' writing as 'Pauline Réage', a preference for anonymity which mirrors that of her heroine – a woman whose name, after all, is a visual representation of zero. That name, according to Aury, was originally Odile and came from a real person. 'But after a few pages I decided that I couldn't do all those things to poor Odile, so I just took the first letter. It has nothing to do with erotic symbolism or the shape of the female sex.' A bizarre coincidence, then? Aury just *happened* to select a name which, when abbreviated, so perfectly expressed her heroine's surrender of desire and will and possibly her life? The notion defies logic, given that Aury's long disappearing act and her heroine's anonymity are entirely congruous with the hole where the novel's heart should be.

For what is conspicuously absent from *Histoire d'O* is the passionate, feeling, desiring female body. O's journey is not simply into sexual slavery but into a condition of acquiescence in which she comes to accept men's desires as her own, first the desires of her lover René and then those of his sinister friend Sir Stephen. Far from being an accident, another of the strange coincidences – like O's name – which Aury would like us to accept, this condition of denial is crucial to the novel's success. Indeed, the book's iconic status can be accounted for in one sentence, which goes like this: *it tells men what they want to hear*. Women exist to be tamed and controlled. There is no need to worry about satisfying them sexually, no anxieties about performance since they will simply accept what they are given, provided the tone in which it is offered is sufficiently masterful. They remain, as Paulhan casually observed in his essay, 'the children we once used to be'. (Although it might be prudent, as he also suggested, to take a whip along in case of trouble when visiting them.)

This tells us a great deal more about male sexual anxiety than it does about female desire; it explains why so many men, to this day, talk about the novel reverently and why so many women dismiss it as silly or irresistibly comic. It does not mean that *Histoire d'O* is wholly dishonest, in spite of Paulhan's and Aury's joint deception, as long as the reader appreciates that the question it addresses is not 'what do women want?' but 'what do men need to believe about women?' The most shocking thing about it, in fact, is that its breathless sado-masochistic fantasies should ever have been mistaken for the authentic voice of female desire, not to mention the depressing fact that its mythology is so well-established that it remains the paradigm for women writing about sex. When the glossy magazine *Tatler* ran a feature in 1995 about the 'quest for the next great erotic novel', approaching five well-known female novelists to come up with synopses, the magazine offered *Histoire d'O* as a model and even made great play of its literary quality. 'In the end', it reassured readers, 'it is not the sexiness of O, but its fine quality that makes the stir so great.' In fact, with its cod eighteenth-century costumes, heaving bosoms and melodramatic swoons – not to mention the aristocratic settings such as the château at Roissy where O is initiated into sexual bondage – it has many of the trappings of the traditional romance novel. (It is also, in the standard English paperback edition, quaintly coy in its use of language. Penetration usually takes place in O's 'belly', and the penis is almost invariably referred to by the bland euphemism 'his sex'.)

What this brings to mind is Virginia Woolf's observation, more than six decades ago, that women are inhibited from writing frankly about their bodies by the knowledge that men would be shocked if they told the truth. Woolf herself seems to have felt the need to come at the subject sideways, placing it near the end of an essay disarmingly entitled 'Professions for Women' which she wrote as a speech to the London/National Society for Women's Service in January 1931. The essay is justly famous for the passage in which Woolf described her struggle to kill the 'Angel in the House', the properly brought-up Victorian girl who peered over her shoulder when she wrote a review of a man's book, urging her to be kind and hide her real feelings. 'Killing the Angel in the House was part of the occupation of a woman writer,' Woolf wrote before going on to consider a task she found even harder: casting off her inhibitions in order to write the truth about her passions. Just how difficult this was, and the extent to which she felt herself to be trespassing on male territory, can be inferred from the image she chose: a young woman novelist who is also 'a fisher*man*' [my italics] sitting on the edge of a deep lake, playing out her line to explore its watery depths which are also a symbol of for the unconscious mind. The writer is in a trance-like state until, all of a sudden:

> The line raced through the girl's fingers. Her imagination had rushed away. It had sought the pools, the depths, the dark places where the largest fish slumber. And then there was a smash. There was an explosion. There was foam and con-fusion. The imagination had dashed itself against something hard. The girl was roused from her dream. She was indeed in a state of the most acute and difficult distress. To speak without figure she had thought of something, something about the body, about the passions which it was unfitting for her as a woman to say. Men, her reason told her, would be shocked. The consciousness of what men will say of a woman who speaks the truth about her passions had roused her from her artist's state of unconsciousness. She could write no more. The

trance was over. Her imagination could work no longer. This I believe to be a very common experience with women writers – they are impeded by the extreme conventionality of the other sex. For though men sensibly allow themselves great freedom in these respects, I doubt that they realize or can control the extreme severity with which they condemn such freedom in women.

Histoire d'O, in spite of its racy reputation, is not the novel to cause such a commotion. Its sexual politics, to use a phrase invented long after Woolf's suicide in 1941, are entirely conventional: Mills & Boon with whips and chains. Virginia Woolf did not think she had solved the problem of 'telling the truth about my own experiences as a body', but she did at least, unlike 'Pauline Réage', understand that there *was* a problem. 'I doubt that any woman has solved it yet,' she added, concluding not very optimistically that 'the obstacles against her are still immensely powerful'.

To argue that this is still the case in the 1990s might appear perverse, given the degree of sexual frankness we are accustomed to in novels, films, even in television drama productions like the plays of Dennis Potter. Yet there is abundant evidence that an essential difference still exists between the way men are permitted to write about sex and what happens when women do it. 'Why have British women writers become so sleazy?' demanded a former literary editor, Graham Lord, in a furious *Daily Mail* article attacking, among others, the prize-winning and strikingly sensual novelist Helen Dunmore. Another author he singled out was Tracy Reed, whose novel *Yellowheart* he characterised as 'the everyday story of an angry, selfish, violent, foul-mouthed nymphomaniac who couples with every man she encounters, even a complete stranger who works in a fast-food van'. This kind of rant, lumping together women novelists of varying calibre and dismissing all of them for daring even to address the subject of sex, is predictable and hardly deserving of a serious response. The furore surrounding *In the Cut*, a frankly erotic novel by the American author Susanna Moore, is altogether more illuminating about taboos and how they operate. Moore's fourth novel took her into the avowedly male territory of serial killers, for, with the exception of the increasingly bizarre Patricia D. Cornwell, such thrillers tend to be the work of men: Thomas Harris, Bret Easton Ellis, Michael Dibdin. *In the Cut* generated a highly charged debate among critics who could not agree whether she was peddling 'designer nihilism', as a reviewer in the *New York Times* claimed, or turning the slice-and-dice genre on its head. They divided sharply over whether *In the Cut* was 'shameless . . . in its depiction of female passivity in the face of ubiquitous male aggression' (Joyce Carol Oates in the *New York Review*) or something altogether more ambitious and complicated.

The novel is about an English teacher called Frannie who lives in an apartment on Washington Square in New York, where a series of brutal sex murders of young women is taking place. (A curious feature of Joyce Carol Oates's hostile review was her insistence on referring to Frannie throughout as X, implying quite wrongly that, like O, she is a woman without even a proper first name.) Frannie has an affair with one of the cops assigned to the case, a coarse, sensual man whom she comes to suspect of being responsible for the murders. It was the graphically described scenes of sex with a possible killer, and Frannie's refusal to alter her way of life in response to the threat, which brought about the charge that she was collusive with the horrible fate that overtakes her at the end of the novel. Moore vehemently denied the accusation, telling the *Observer*:

Frannie is a woman who refuses the powerlessness imposed on her. She is told that life must be less adventurous, erotic, curious. She takes risks in order to be free. I wanted to ask what being a woman in a big city at the end of the century means.

I think when people say that Frannie's a masochist, it's because we have allowed ourselves to believe that we deserve the things that are done to us. Frannie resists her fate every inch of the way. Literally and metaphorically, she tries not to die. Her avidity and eagerness are about not dying.

The point about *In the Cut*, which many critics seemed to miss, is that it is essentially a novel about language. Moore's attempt to discover a vocabulary of sex for her heroine which avoids the clichés and imprecisions of *Histoire d'O* (and she succeeds stunningly, as several female critics pointed out) is paralleled by Frannie's project of compiling a dictionary of slang; although this is superficially an investigation into black and working-class language, it really amounts to a glossary of how *men* speak. Moore's contention is that male language conflates sex and violence to such a degree – hence 'in the cut', a reference to the vagina whose association with slashing is painfully obvious – that her heroine cannot tell whether her lover is lying to her because he still has sex with his wife or because he is the killer.

In that sense, *In the Cut* is about a woman trying to listen to her own body and decode an alien, verbal language at the same time. Unlike *Histoire d'O*, it does not pretend that men do terrible things to women because they like them: 'Do you know what's ridiculous? How much women love men, we're crazy about them. But men are terrified of women, full of fear and loathing,' Moore has said. Her novel suggests that men are afraid of women's desire, and of their own. Yet – and this is where it differs radically from *Histoire d'O* and from Frank Wedekind's 'Lulu' plays – she is clear that this is no more women's fault than death is the concealed aim of their sexuality. For the actress Louise Brooks, who played Lulu in the most famous film version of *Pandora's Box*, the character was not only collusive in but longed for her own annihilation: 'It is Christmas Eve,' Brooks said, describing the film's spine-chilling denouement, 'and [Lulu] is about to receive the gift that has been her dream since childhood: death by a sexual maniac.' By contrast, Susanna Moore's Frannie wants to have sexual pleasure *and* live. The horrifying ending of *In the Cut*, painfully hard as it is to read, suggests that the compatibility of those aims cannot be taken for granted.

In the spring of 1996, around the time Moore's novel was making such a stir, a case came to court in California involving the singer Madonna. Someone claiming to be a fan, a man named Robert Hoskins, had repeatedly tried to make contact with the star, finally breaking into the grounds of her home and being shot by one of her bodyguards. Hoskins was charged under anti-stalking legislation and Madonna was summoned, against her will, to give evidence at his trial; Hoskins, said one of her aides, had thus achieved his aim of forcing her to face him in person. Although it was clear that Hoskins had waged a campaign of terror against her, for which he was sent to prison, journalists insinuated that Madonna had somehow invited the attention of a deranged and dangerous fan, or belittled the incident by suggesting that a stalker was merely the latest fashionable accessory for a superstar. Yet what the trial actually demonstrated was the degree of risk faced by a woman who dares to present herself in public as a desiring, unashamedly sexual being. Madonna is not the first female star to attract the attention of a stalker, but her decade-long career provides a paradigm of the responses, ranging from overt threat to ridicule, which women encounter when they assert themselves sexually.

Ever since the release of her first single, 'Like a Virgin', Madonna has played with and challenged traditional ideas about femininity. Her avowed aim of being Marilyn-Monroe-with-power raised the question of whether vulnerability remains an indivisible element of that particular package, and her voyeuristic *Sex* book prompted, as well as mockery, serious questions about the extent to which her explorations of the erotic were stuck in a de Sadeian, anti-Catholic tradition. Musically she was much more bold and innovative, especially on the *Erotica* CD which took on themes as varied as sexual jealousy, emotional sadism and the pleasures of *cunnilingus*. Inevitably, though, the twists and turns in her career were met with ridicule of a very particular sort, namely the accusation that her enthusiasm for sex had put off so many men that she could not find anyone to go out with her. This stereotype, which is frequently employed against women with an enviably high and sexy public profile, was visible in full force in a *Daily Mail* article in the spring of 1996 which purported to reveal, in tones of mock-sympathy, that Madonna had become an isolated, frustrated figure. 'Although the superstar is surrounded by servants and adoring fans,' the paper reported, 'her biggest problem is loneliness.' Under the headline 'In bed with Madonna? Here's why Englishmen would really rather not', the paper listed the rebuffs she had supposedly received from half a dozen famous men, including the actor Hugh Grant and Madness singer Graham McPherson. The double-page spread

129

made a point of recalling that Rupert Everett, with whom she had enjoyed a 'long-standing friendship', had recently revealed his homosexuality, while another ex-boyfriend, Old Etonian property developer Mungo Tennant, was quoted as saying 'there was no attraction on my side really'. Madonna's biographer Douglas Thompson joined in, telling the *Mail*:

> Madonna sits in her pristine, highly-polished home after the servants have gone home surfing the TV channels. It's her way of socialising. It's almost a fantasy for her – imagining a love affair with all the British actors she sees on TV.

The subtext is clear enough: poor little rich girl flaunts her body but can't find a man who's interested in it. The newspaper did make an attempt to be even-handed, quoting a British journalist based in Los Angeles who suggested that Madonna's upfront, very American brand of sexuality might have scared off some of the men she was said to have approached. But the overall message of the piece was spelled out in a strapline across the top of both pages: 'Despite her persistence, the Material Girl's penchant for British men has failed to land a lasting relationship'. It was clear that readers were not being asked to feel sorry for Madonna so much as gloat over her sexual and romantic failures – a classic example of *Schadenfreude*.

This was even more frankly spelled out by one of the newspaper's columnists, the former *Sunday Times* editor Andrew Neil, when he tackled the same story. Neil's central conceit – in both senses – was a pretence that he was living in fear of a call from the star. 'Madonna is gaining quite a reputation for cold-calling any man she fancies,' he wrote, describing the prospect of an approach as 'the call from hell'. Her latest 'victim' was *Middlemarch* star Rufus Sewell, who had agreed to have dinner with her but left after the first course. 'I fear that Madonna is getting increasingly desperate,' Neil concluded. 'I'm keeping my answering-machine on to screen incoming calls. I advise all male readers (maybe female ones, too) to do the same until further notice.'

Even when Madonna announced a few months later that she was pregnant – incontrovertible proof that she had, in tabloid terms, got herself a man – newspapers implied that her choice of partner (not a famous name, nor indeed a suave English public school boy, but her personal trainer) demonstrated her unpopularity and isolation. It was almost a replay of what happened in 1991, when the *Sex* book was published to widespread derision and Madonna eventually came back fighting with a song, 'Human Nature', on her *Bedtime Stories* CD. On that occasion, clearly stung, she accused her critics of trying to prevent her talking about sex – effectively to silence her. What she had not yet grasped – and whether she has by now taken the lesson to heart remains to be seen – is an unpalatable fact about women and sexuality. The Victorians were far from alone in wanting to believe that women are constitutionally less sexual than men, that the poet Coleridge was correct in his *ex cathedra* pronouncement that a woman's desire 'is rarely other than for the desire of a man'. Rape fantasies and romance apart, at the end of the twentieth century female desire is still the love that dare not speak its name.

Unnatural Born Killers

ROSE AND MYRA, Myra and Rose. Immediately after Rosemary West was given a record number of life sentences for murder at Winchester Crown Court in November 1995, the tabloids reported that she had been seen holding hands, in the high-security wing of Durham prison, with her predecessor as Britain's most hated woman. 'Rose's pact of friendship with Hindley' was the headline in the *Daily Express*, over a short article claiming that 'the women are said to have been drawn together by their love of religion'. According to unnamed 'sources', they had made 'unsupervised visits to each other's cells and have prayed together in the jail chapel'. The friendship flourished 'when West began to confide in Hindley, who later assumed the role of adviser'. The subtext was clear: not just the women's nauseating hypocrisy in their public display of religious observance but the irresistible image of depraved Rosemary West sitting obediently at the feet of her evil mentor, the child-killer Myra Hindley. It hardly mattered whether the story was true or not, for tabloid logic demanded the pairing of these two supremely wicked women: Nightmare on Cromwell Street meets The White Devil. (The newspaper was later censured, however, by the body responsible for handling complaints against the press.)

The day before the article appeared, the police had released a colour photograph of Rosemary West for use on television and in the next day's newspapers. Rightly judging that the case would receive saturation coverage, especially in the tabloids – the *Daily Express* devoted fourteen pages to 'the full horrific story', for once relegating the latest round in the Prince and

Princess of Wales's marital conflict to a mere two – the police photographer had snapped West full-face, staring expressionlessly into the camera, in an obvious echo of the infamous mugshot of the Moors Murderess. Yet while West had just been found guilty of some of the most horrific crimes ever described in British judicial proceedings, her picture was something of a disappointment; this was no Hindley, all bleached blonde hair and pitiless lips, but a middle-aged woman with badly cut brown hair and old-fashioned glasses. Where Hindley appeared a woman of her time in the photograph taken shortly after her arrest in 1965, hard as nails and icily sexy, Rosemary West was plump and homely, someone who wouldn't attract attention in a crowd of mothers waiting for their children at the school gate. The picture was unpromising material for anyone trying to explain how this 41-year-old mother of eight came to take part in the torture and murder of young women and girls; forced to abandon the 'face of evil' line relentlessly pursued in the long aftermath of the Moors Murders, journalists divided into two camps. Some, like the *Daily Mirror*'s columnist Paul Callan, resorted to simple abuse; West stood in the dock, he averred, 'like a toad on a stone, her face visibly paling'. When the judge pronounced sentence, 'her normally mean mouth tightened like a zipped purse and she turned briskly on her right heel. There was even a hint of defiance in the way she walked from the dock, with the two lady [sic] warders close behind her.'

Mean, unrepentant, defiant to the end; elsewhere in the *Daily Mirror*, feature writer Cheryl Stonehouse tried and failed to discern these very same characteristics. Rosemary West was a woman 'sunk so deep in depravity and brutality that she is unique. Yet you could never tell by looking at her.' Below a colour graphic caricaturing West as a spider – the black widow – at the centre of her web, Stonehouse wrote:

Here is a plump, middle-aged woman. Living in a peaceful part of England. With a daily routine like millions of others.

See her in the supermarket. See her in the street. See her with her children. Just an ordinary wife and mother.

No one except her husband saw the real Rose West. Few of us could even imagine her evil.

Nevertheless, according to an unsigned article in the *Daily Star*, this unremarkable Gloucester housewife had succeeded in dislodging Hindley from her previously unchallenged position 'as Britain's most hated serial killer'. While it is obviously true that Rosemary West's homely appearance sits uneasily with the story that unfolded over the eight weeks of her trial, which was a sickening catalogue of abduction, calculated sexual abuse, mutilation and murder, it is generally the case that serial killers are undistinguished in the flesh, bearing little resemblance to the monsters popular sentiment would like them to resemble. Robert Wilson, then an evening newspaper journalist in the north of England, already knew that Ian Brady and Myra Hindley were implicated in the abduction and murder of two children, and the death of a teenage boy, when he got his first sight of them at their committal hearing in 1965. But the couple were not at all what he expected:

> They stood before the world, he, flanked by two policemen, she by two policewomen. I stared at them, puzzled. There had been some mistake, the police must have got the wrong people. That isn't Ian Brady. That isn't Myra Hindley. I still don't know what I expected. But I had never expected this.
> *They looked human.*

Wilson was still mesmerised by their unexceptional appearance when he wrote a book about the Moors Murders two decades later. Brady and Hindley were 'typical of thousands of young couples you might see together, sitting holding hands in a cinema, smooching on the dance floor at the Ashton Palais', he admitted. In this respect, plain, ordinary Rosemary West is no different from dozens of other murderers; if she is a troubling addition to the roll-call of serial killers which has become an unwelcome but familiar litany of our century, it is not because of her appearance. Nor, indeed, is it the number of her crimes that makes her stand out. Peter Sutcliffe was convicted of killing thirteen women in the north of England and attacking another seven; Dennis Nilsen murdered and dismembered fifteen young men he had lured back to his flat in London with the offer of a bed for the night. In the United States, John Wayne Gacy was executed for the murder and mutilation of thirty-two boys and young men; Ted Bundy is believed to have bludgeoned to death nearly forty women.

Sutcliffe, Nilsen, Gacy, Bundy, Albert DeSalvo, John Christie, Neville Heath, Peter Kürten, David Berkowitz, Henry Lee Lucas, Carlton Gary, Bobby Joe Long, Jeffrey Dahmer, Kenneth Erskine, Michael Lupo, Colin Ireland; in what the author Colin Wilson has called 'the age of sex crime', we have become accustomed to their names and the dreadful catalogue of brutality associated with them. We are also aware, at some level, of the fact that they are all men. 'There are no known cases in which a serial killer is a female,' the criminologist Steven Egger wrote bluntly in 1984. He also pointed out that 'in a preponderance of known cases, the victims are young females chosen to satisfy the lust of the serial murderer'. With very rare exceptions like the English nurse who was found guilty of killing several of her infant patients, this formulation remains broadly true to this day, revealing a stark and inescapable asymmetry: serial killing is, in a majority of cases, a crime in which men are the perpetrators and women the victims. This uncomfortable fact may go some way towards explaining the widespread tendency to glamorise serial killers, to move them from the real world of pain, blood and guts into a semi-mythic realm where they are identified by pantomimic nicknames: Jack the Ripper, the Boston Strangler, the Night Stalker, the Green River Killer. Once this transfer to the symbolic realm is complete, they can even become heroes. The German dramatist Frank Wedekind finished the first of his two 'Lulu' plays, *Erdgeist* (*Earth Spirit*), in 1895, only seven years after the original Ripper murders in the East End of London which are said to have been his inspiration; his heroine, whose cold, glittering sexuality ensnares and destroys one man after another, finally turns to prostitution and, in *Die Büchse der Pandora* (*Pandora's Box*), dies at the hands of a client who turns out to be none other than Jack. (This combination, Lulu and the Ripper, was so seductive that Wedekind's plays had already been filmed four times when the German movie director G. W. Pabst cast the American actress Louise Brooks as the seductress/victim in his eerie and compelling post-expressionist film *Pandora's Box* in 1928. Alban Berg's adaptation of both plays into an opera, simply entitled *Lulu*, was first performed in the 1930s and remains popular to this day.)

Charles McCabe, a columnist on the *San Francisco Chronicle*, notoriously saluted Jack the Ripper as 'that great hero of my youth, that skilled butcher who did all his work on alcoholic whores'. Robert Bloch, author of *Psycho*, urged his readers to 'let the Ripper rip you into an awareness of the urges and forces most of us will neither admit nor submit to'. In a symbiotic process, 'Jack' has enjoyed a long and varied career in films and novels, while fictional serial killers such as Hannibal Lecter, the psychiatrist turned anthropophagic murderer from Thomas Harris's accomplished thrillers *Red Dragon* and *The Silence of the Lambs*, have become archetypes of the hero/villain who enthralls both Hollywood and the popular imagination (Lecter has already appeared in two movies, played by Brian Cox in Michael Mann's stylish *Manhunter* and Anthony Hopkins in Jonathan Demme's version of *The Silence of the Lambs*).

Because the victims of so many serial killers, from Jack the Ripper onwards, have been female, the theory has frequently been advanced that serial murderers live with smothering mothers and hate them so much that they are compelled ritually to destroy them over and over again. This theory has an obvious flaw, as Professor David Canter pointed out in his book *Criminal Shadows: Inside the Mind of the Serial Killer*. Canter, who is head of the Liverpool University investigative psychology unit, asked rhetorically: 'Why do we get no women serial killers living with their over-indulgent, elderly fathers?' The truth is that while the numbers of serial killers have been increasing exponentially – from 644 individual murders in the United States in 1966 to an estimated 4,118 in 1982, according to the FBI – their motivation is still poorly understood. And when we are faced with a criminal like Rosemary West, who deviates in almost every respect from the prevailing notion of a serial killer, such theories are worse than useless. She is the wrong gender, not a loner but a married woman living in an unusually populous household, variously described as a cheap lodging-house and a brothel; detectives investigating the case have apparently identified 150 people who passed through 25 Cromwell Street during the Wests' residence there, staying for periods as short as two or three days or as long as several years. But there is another factor which complicates the West case, perhaps fatally damaging our chances of gaining an insight into how and indeed if she became a murderer – the prosecution case against her was by no means proved – and that is the suicide in prison of her husband, the builder Frederick West. By standing trial alone, Rosemary West's case can be manipulated to foster the myth not of the lone female serial killer – the most dramatic way of redressing the alarming gender imbalance described above – but of the next best thing, a murderous relationship between a man and a woman in which the latter is the driving force. It is this impulse which lies behind the concerted attempt, in the aftermath of the trial, to suggest that the Cromwell Street murders marked the moment when Britain finally achieved the dubious distinction of having a female Jack the Ripper.

The rush to present the Cromwell Street murders in this light was predictable and immediate. In the final week of the trial Colin Wilson confidently asserted on BBC Radio Four's *Today* programme that Rosemary West had gradually become the dominant partner in the couple's crimes, a claim as unsubstantiated as his observation in the same interview that her husband's murderous proclivities were the result of a head injury. The notion of Rosemary West as the dominant personality was echoed by the *Daily Telegraph*, which characterised her immediately after the trial as 'the strategist behind her moronic, doting husband'. The newspaper repeated the claim elsewhere in its coverage of the case, in almost identical words: 'Rosemary was the dominant partner, people said, the strategist.'

Quite how 'people' knew this, when the evidence of an unprecedented number of witnesses was tainted by cash offers from the media of up to £100,000, is not easy to establish. But it is worth pointing out that in January 1995, immediately after Frederick West hanged himself in prison, the Crown Prosecution Service expressed public doubts about whether there was sufficient evidence for the case against his widow to proceed. 'West's wife may go free' was the headline in the London *Evening Standard*, over a story which stated unequivocally: 'The Crown Prosecution

Service today gave a clear indication that the case against Rosemary West could collapse following her husband's suicide.' An unnamed spokesman for the CPS confirmed that 'we will have to see if there is enough evidence for a realistic chance of prosecution and whether it is in the public interest to do so'. Indeed, Frederick West's suicide landed the CPS with a particularly awkward problem in relation to Charmaine, the seven-year-old daughter of his first wife, Rena (Catherine) Costello. The date of the child's disappearance and death could not be pinpointed with accuracy, but it happened some time in 1971, when Frederick spent the first half of the year in prison. Certainly Charmaine was alive at the end of April, when the last photograph of her was taken; assuming that Frederick killed her some time after his release from prison on 24 June – dental examinations gave uncertain results, suggesting a date of death between the end of June and the end of July – the CPS duly charged him with the murder. Rosemary, who had been jointly charged with nine murders, was *not* charged on this count. Yet twelve days after her husband's suicide, and a full eight months after charges were originally laid against her, the murder of Charmaine was abruptly added to the indictment. Brian Masters, whose book *'She Must Have Known': The Trial of Rosemary West* examines the evidence against her in minute detail, asks why the police had been prepared to see Frederick West go to trial for a murder which, they now decided, he could *not* have committed because he was in prison at the time. The reason, Masters suggests, is that linking Rosemary to Charmaine's death was vital to the case against *her*: 'if it could be shown that she was responsible for this death . . . then the imputation that she was involved in the other murders would be more difficult to resist with or without evidence.' The last two words are crucial; even the *Daily Telegraph*'s own post-trial analysis, which was structured around the notion that Rosemary was the dominant partner in both the marriage and the murders, had to admit that the West case was 'a prosecution brought without any direct evidence of the defendant's part in the crimes with which she was charged'.

The jury was aware of this unusual feature of the case. Shortly before it reached verdicts on the remaining seven charges – Rosemary West had been found guilty on three counts, including the murder of Charmaine, the day before – its members returned to court to ask the judge a startling question: 'Is *the total absence of direct evidence* other than the presence of the remains linking the victims to 25 Cromwell Street an obstruction to bringing in a guilty verdict?' (my italics). The judge advised that it was not, providing the jury could draw the necessary inferences on the evidence put forward by the prosecution. Not long afterwards, the jury returned with 'guilty' verdicts on all the outstanding charges.

None of this is to excuse or exonerate Rosemary West, whose character was comprehensively destroyed during the court case and whose brutal treatment of surviving victims like Caroline Owens – sexually molested by Rosemary, raped by Frederick, threatened and then set free – beggars belief. But Rosemary West's husband is dead, and as long as she continues to protest her innocence it is hard to come to any reliable conclusion about the respective roles they played. What evidence there is from previous cases – and they form a minute subsection in the documented history of serial killers – is of a pattern in which a young and impressionable woman falls under the influence of a dominant older man.

'Typically in these events, the man is the leader and the woman is playing to that,' David Canter observed after Rosemary West's trial. Helena Kennedy QC made the same point slightly differently in her book *Eve Was Framed: Women and British Justice*. 'On the few occasions when women have played a role in serial killings, as in the Moors and Manson murders, they have functioned as hand maidens to a master,' she wrote. What is remarkable about the West trial is just how swiftly the role reversal took place in the public mind, dramatically shifting the spotlight from the man, who admitted to all the crimes with which he was charged, to the woman who did not. The same process, which eventually resulted in the demonising of Myra Hindley to the near-exclusion of Ian Brady, took significantly longer in the Moors Murders case; it was broadly accepted at the trial in 1966 and for some time after that Hindley, four years younger than Brady, was very much the junior partner in their crimes. Helena Kennedy has pointed out that Hindley was represented in contemporaneous press reports as Brady's 'sex slave', and that there was little doubt that 'she was not the prime mover in the murders'. Evidence emerged at the trial that Brady had induced her to share two of his long-standing obsessions, the Third Reich and the works of the Marquis de Sade. The author Emlyn Williams, in his book *Beyond Belief*, explicitly suggests that there was a sado-masochistic relationship between them, citing photographs of Hindley which reveal the marks of a whip:

> In two of the single female poses, the model is completely nude; in the one she lies on the floor, face downwards and head away from the camera, feet together in the foreground, in the other the same position except that she is kneeling. On the buttocks, in both poses, several very faint horizontal lines. In the corner, the dangling end of a knotted whip.

Brady, originally convicted of three murders to Hindley's two, has all but disappeared from the public consciousness; Frederick West's suicide opened the way for a similar change in perception in relation to the Cromwell Street murders. Yet the notion of Frederick West as the dupe of his scheming second wife sits uneasily with the fact that he had committed at least one murder, and possibly two, before he even met her.

The chronology, like much else in the case, is not entirely clear. But Frederick West's first victim, Anne McFall, was last seen in the summer of 1967, two years *before* he met Rosemary Letts (at the time of the disappearance, Frederick's future wife was a thirteen-year-old schoolgirl). Anne, who had worked as a nanny for West and his first wife, Rena, was heavily pregnant with his child – as Shirley Robinson would be when she was killed more than ten years later. Anne's body, along with the bones of her unborn baby, was later found by police in Fingerpost Field, Much Marcle, the village where Frederick West grew up. Rena West disappeared some time after Anne McFall – at one point, Frederick confessed to killing Rena in a field, realising her daughter Charmaine was still in his car and going back to dispose of the child – and her remains were also found near Much Marcle. David Canter has pointed out that the first murder in a series often involves a member of the family or friend who is killed for relatively mundane reasons such as anger, frustration, jealousy or to conceal a crime – a pattern to which the murders of Anne McFall and Rena West apparently conform. West's reckless disregard for the law is reflected in his initial dealings with Rosemary Letts, who was only fifteen years old when he picked her up at a bus stop and began an illicit sexual relationship with her in 1969. Indeed, there is a striking parallel between Rosemary at this age and some of the girls and young women who would later become the couple's victims. Like them, she was a vulnerable adolescent from an unstable background; according to the *Evening Standard*, minor transgressions in the Letts family 'were punished with beatings and the children's fear of their father's temper was shared by their mother, whom neighbours recall once being dragged into the street by her hair'. Rosemary's younger brother recalled his father doing 'awful things to my mum'.

At the time of their first meeting, Frederick West was twenty-seven, nearly twice Rosemary's age; it is hard not to construe his relationship with her as abusive. (His own childhood, living in rural poverty with parents who imposed discipline through regular beatings and in an atmosphere where incest seems to have been tolerated, was hardly designed to instil a grasp of conventional sexual boundaries. This textbook abuser's background throws an almost comic light on the *Daily Star*'s pompous assertion, in an editorial, that 'the West case does not teach us any lessons about our society'.) 'We couldn't understand what a man with two children wanted with a fifteen-year-old child,' said Rosemary's mother, Daisy, after the trial, displaying astonishing naivety. Rosemary later claimed she had already been raped twice by strangers when she met Frederick, who wooed her with a second-hand fur coat and a lace dress. Within months she was pregnant; her parents put her into care and urged her to have an abortion, but her sixteenth birthday intervened and she moved into a cramped, dirty caravan with Frederick and his daughters.

The couple's first child, Heather, was born in Midland Road, Gloucester, in 1970, by which time Frederick and Rosemary were already encouraging teenage girls to take part in sex sessions. David Canter has suggested that the couple probably told each other their victims enjoyed the sexual ordeals they put them through: 'My guess is that the Wests would have discussed it with themselves along the lines of everybody having a good time,' he said. What happened next may never be known for certain, although the prosecution's case that Rosemary decided, off her own bat, to kill Charmaine while her husband was in prison, then kept the body for him to dispose of when he emerged, does rather stretch credulity. After that, also according to the prosecution, the couple's murder spree got going in earnest, sometimes involving victims who had been drawn to the lodging-house-cum-brothel in Cromwell Street, sometimes girls picked up away from the house – although it is worth noting that the Crown was unable to prove that Rosemary West had even met six of the victims whose bodies were buried in the house and its environs.

Lynda Gough, nineteen, vanished in April 1973 after moving into Cromwell Street to look after the West children. Fifteen-year-old Carol Ann Cooper, who had been taken into care by Worcestershire County Council, was last seen getting on a bus in November that year. Lucy Partington, a 21-year-old student, disappeared a month later after visiting a friend in Cheltenham. Therese Siegenthaler, a Swiss student, vanished in April 1974 after setting out to hitch-hike to Wales and take a ferry to Ireland. Fifteen-year-old Shirley Hubbard disappeared in November that year after leaving the Debenhams store in Worcester where she was doing work experience. Juanita Mott, eighteen, lodged at Cromwell Street and was not seen again after April 1975. Four years later seventeen-year-old Alison Chambers failed to turn up for work. The couple's own daughter, Heather, disappeared in June 1987 when she was sixteen. The final victim was Shirley Robinson, eighteen and eight months pregnant with Frederick's child, who vanished in May 1978. The remains of all eight were found at Cromwell Street.

The natural human reaction to the account in Winchester Crown Court of what happened to these girls and women is one of sick horror. Many people simply stopped reading reports of the trial, unable to stomach the picture which was emerging, although it has to be said that the tabloids were probably correct in their estimation that an avid audience was waiting for the sordid revelations they had in store after Rosemary West's conviction.

The *Daily Mirror* shamelessly printed a secondhand account of Frederick West's unsubstantiated claim that 'he and his evil wife Rose belonged to a band of sex fiends called The Cult who slaughtered TWENTY girls'. Its front-page headline 'My Cult Will Kill Again' was surreally juxtaposed with an offer of a free Christmas and New Year TV Guide, with 'your full festive listings'.

The problem with this approach, apart from the minor matter of taste, is that it transforms tragic crimes into a horror movie scenario. The air of unreality introduced into the proceedings is not just an insult to the victims but a serious obstruction to any real understanding of the case; among the things we do know about serial killers is that they are not charismatic characters like Hannibal the Cannibal or the fiendishly cunning Temple Brooks Gault, boldly hacking into the FBI's computers, in Patricia D. Cornwell's best-selling forensic thrillers. Even the term 'serial killer' is unhelpful; as David Canter has emphasised, it is not the fact that they repeat their crimes that marks these criminals out. Most lawbreakers, from burglars to car thieves to credit card fraudsters, are stuck in a cycle of repetition. Indeed, there is a sense in which murder, for these multiple killers, is merely a by-product of or an attempt to conceal the purpose for which they selected their victims in the first place. What distinguishes serial killers is a catastrophic inability to make healthy adult relationships: unable to see other people as fully human, they treat them as objects to be used, exploited and disposed of at will. The mutilation which follows death, as well as aiding disposal, is a graphic illustration of the way in which the victims have been dehumanised. This is the real, abiding horror of the serial killer: chronically insecure, they enjoy the sensation of having others in their power. In the West case, the victims seem to have been kept alive, bound and gagged, for up to days at a time; Peter Sutcliffe, the Yorkshire Ripper, projected on to women's bodies the weakness he feared in himself; Jeffrey Dahmer, a lonely white man, murdered and occasionally ate the black and South-East Asian men he picked up in bars in Milwaukee, thus literally incorporating the feared and desired 'other'. But the sense of power they gain from subduing and exploiting their victims is only temporary. All their relationships end in death, a chilling reminder of their underlying inadequacy which explains why men like Ian Brady and Frederick West seek a partner in crime.

'To do something as vile as what was going on with somebody you know who tolerates it is a form of egging on,' David Canter has observed. What the women get out of it is a feeling of being elevated above the rest of their sex, presumably a heady sensation for a disturbed fifteen-year-old like Rosemary Letts. 'Some women', Helena Kennedy suggested in *Eve Was Framed*, 'feel strangely flattered at being chosen by such men, as though they had been singled out from the ordinary run of womankind' – a point Emily Brontë makes in that most savage of novels, *Wuthering Heights*. Heathcliff, expressing his disgust for his estranged wife, Isabella, recalls the brutality he openly displayed on the night of their elopement. His denunciation of her is couched in terms that might equally apply to a serial killer's female accomplice:

> She cannot accuse me of showing a bit of deceitful softness. The first thing she saw me do, on coming out of the Grange, was to hang up her little dog, and when she pleaded for it, the first words I uttered were a wish that I had the hanging of every being belonging to her, except one: possibly she took that exception for herself – But no brutality disgusted her – I suppose she has an innate admiration of it, if only her precious person were secure from injury! Now, was it not the depth of absurdity – of genuine idiocy, for that pitiful, slavish, mean-minded brach to dream that I could love her? Tell your master, Nelly, that I never, in all my life, met with such an abject thing as she is –

Heathcliff, in spite of his inherent sadism, is persistently read by teenage girls – and older women who should know better – as a romantic hero. Myra Hindley's diary, written at the time she met Brady at work, has been described by Helena Kennedy as 'a catalogue of childish desperation for him to show some interest in her'. Excerpts from it, reprinted in *Beyond Belief*, include such naive sentiments as 'I am in a bad mood because he hasn't spoken to me today' and 'I hope he loves me and will marry me some day'. When Frederick West was in prison for theft in 1971, his wife wrote him sentimental, adoring letters; Frederick's daughter Anne-Marie, who was raped by her father with her stepmother's encouragement, said that the couple 'doted on each other. Rosemary had so much love for my dad. She would have done anything for him . . .' A more sinister light is thrown on the couple's relationship by documents in Rosemary's handwriting, quoted in Brian Masters's book, which suggest that she was, like Hindley, a species of sex slave. One, countersigned by Frederick West, reads:

> I, Rose, will do exactly what I am told, when I am told, without questions, without losing my temper, for a period of three months from the end of my next period, as I think I owe this to Fred.

The other, so unpleasant that Masters could not bring himself to quote it in full, begins 'I, Rosemary West, known as Fred's cow' and lists the orifices which she will make available to her husband on request.

What kind of cultural contortion is required to turn these unequal partnerships, Fred-and-Rose and Ian-and-Myra, into narratives of *female* domination? How does fifteen-year-old Rosemary Letts, seduced with cheap gifts by a man almost twice her age – already a fully-fledged murderer in his own right – mutate into a criminal mastermind, manipulating her doltish husband? Helena Kennedy, writing before the Cromwell Street murders came to light, suggested that a woman like Myra Hindley 'is the vessel into which society pours its dark secrets; like a war criminal, such a "she-devil" is a reminder of what is horribly possible'. Of course Kennedy is right; offending against popular notions of womanhood as protective and nurturing, the transgressions of Myra Hindley serve to confirm, in a perverse way, the very norms from which they deviate. But an even more complex ritual is being played out in our response to these ghastly cases, as the aftermath of the West trial makes clear.

Female killers are simultaneously hate-objects who maintain other women in their customary beatific light and Lady Macbeths who incarnate men's darkest fears and desires: when a woman is bad, she is far, far worse than a man could ever be. ('The female of the species is more deadly than the male,' as Kipling once claimed.) Yet criminal history shows that the dominant female killer, luring her hapless male partner into crimes he would never for a moment have contemplated committing without her evil prompting, is a myth; we believe in her not because she exists but because, like children who refuse to give up their attachment to Father Christmas, we need her too much to allow inconvenient reality to get in the way. For thirty years, the White Devil held centre stage, her performance tending towards but never quite achieving perfection; now, with the arrival of the Black Widow, the apotheosis is complete. With their pathetic male accomplices relegated to the wings, languishing in the shadows of madness and death, the true partners-in-crime are revealed in all their malignant glory. Here they come, hand in hand, that demonic *female* duo: Myra-and-Rose.

Part III

Making a Difference

Five Propositions and a Conclusion

MEN AND WOMEN ARE different. Everyone knows that. They have different physiques, different sex organs, they play different roles in reproduction and they wear different clothes. All right, the clothes thing isn't a genuine difference, but it does represent a cultural acknowledgement of the asymmetry of the two sexes. As Matt Ridley writes in his influential book *The Red Queen*, 'conditioning usually reinforces instinct rather than overrides it'; dressing little girls in frilly party frocks isn't a way of imposing femininity on them, it's simply encouraging what's already there. Why, then, did women suddenly start to rebel in the 1960s against the strict sartorial rules which said only men should wear trousers? Or that women couldn't buy drinks in pint glasses? To many observers, women who insisted on being allowed to wear jeans to work like men, and girls who wanted to wear trousers at school like boys, were making a fuss about nothing. Did it really matter if women were expected, in certain circumstances, to put on a skirt? For Ridley, these protests were all part of 'the great human experiment called the 1960s' in which 'much conditioning was rejected yet the pattern survives'. Men and women *are* different, and no amount of tinkering with secondary sexual characteristics can get away from that fact. Look at the insidious influence of our different reproductive roles, whose contrasting sexual aims have had a profound impact not just on our attitudes to sex but on the way we organise our lives. Ridley suggests, following the biologist Robert Trivers's argument in his 1972 essay 'Parental Investment and Sexual Selection', that fidelity to a single partner (monogamy) suits women, who can bear the offspring of only one man at a time, while having multiple partners (polygamy) works better for men, who are biologically programmed to impregnate as many women as possible. Ridley's own chapter on this subject in *The Red Queen* is uncompromisingly titled 'Polygamy and the Nature of Men', and it insists not once but several times that 'males are generally seducers and females the seduced', a division of sexual labour which he sees mirrored in the customs which govern marriage proposals:

> Even among the most liberated of westerners, men are expected to ask and women to answer. The tradition of women asking men on Leap Year's Day reinforces the very paucity of their opportunities: they get one day to pop the question for every 1460 that men can do so. It is true that many modern men do not go down upon one knee, but 'discuss' the matter with their girlfriends as equals. Yet even so, the subject is usually first raised by the man. And in the matter of seduction itself, once more it is the male that is expected to make the first move. Women may flirt, but men pounce.

Does this picture of contemporary society strike you as, shall we say, a little out of date? Ridley's book was published in 1993, when the unprecedented unpopularity of marriage in Western Europe was already worrying traditionalists; it has been obvious for some time that 'the most liberated of westerners' are no longer getting married at all. As I have already shown in these pages, almost a third of children born in Britain in recent years have parents who are not married; in Scandinavia, it is around half. Men *and* women are trying out a variety of ways of organising their lives, and the only discernible pattern is a move towards serial relationships. Does this mean that biology has, after thousands of years, suddenly loosened its grip? A more convincing explanation is that Ridley's old-fashioned fantasy of rugged men popping the question to blushing maidens is a reflection not so much of biological imperatives as an archaic power imbalance, originating in men's superior physical strength and women's inability until very recently to avoid pregnancy, which has finally broken down.

It is certainly the case that while Ridley presents himself as a rationalist, sifting evidence and rejecting fanciful explanations of human behaviour, his arguments are undermined by his reliance on antiquated and unsupported assumptions. Take his assertion that men make the first move in sexual relationships – a fine example, if ever there was one, of what I have come to think of as the pathetic phallacy. To inject a personal note for a moment, in my experience it's more like half and half. What planet has Ridley been living on for the past few years?

This book is about precisely that kind of assumption, glibly expressed but seldom examined, about the differences between men and women. In the first section, about the women whose images continue to beguile us, I examined the extent to which we reward traditionally 'feminine' behaviour, whether it manifests itself in the Princess of Wales's canny presentation of herself as a beautiful, wronged, suffering woman or in the re-inscription of biology – motherhood – as the defining test of what it takes to be a woman. In the second section, about the women we fear and despise, I looked at the many ways in which women are punished for deviating from that narrowly defined concept of proper female conduct. What I have been suggesting is that there are many more rules governing female behaviour than men's, and that it is consequently much harder for a woman, however strong-minded she is, to be an individual – to act on her own desires and ambitions – rather than conforming to the expectations heaped on her from birth.

In this final section, I am going to present five propositions and a conclusion which seem to me to emerge naturally from this book. My starting-point, that the difference between the sexes has been exaggerated for most of recorded history, is a minority view – but no more subjective than many other supposedly 'scientific' or unbiased accounts. The first and in many ways most significant of these propositions is that *the main difference between men and women in any culture is that women are treated differently*. What I mean by this is that most of what we think of as essential differences between the sexes are actually the result of imposing different conditions on men and women, whether it is in superficial matters like appearance or a question of the opportunities made available to them. Here is a simple example: when I was at a single-sex state grammar school in the late 1960s, we were encouraged (and I strenuously refused) to take A levels in subjects like anatomy, physiology and hygiene. One of the subjects that attracted me, economics, simply wasn't taught at my school, although it was on offer at the boys' grammar school on the other side of town. This difference in the curriculum had nothing to do with innate abilities or inclinations – I still regret knowing so little about economics – and everything to do with what was thought suitable for girls. But our resulting ignorance of this important subject could be, and I'm sure was, interpreted as saying something about our intellectual capacity in comparison with boys.

A much more dramatic and shocking example of what I'm talking about happened in Kabul, the capital of Afghanistan, when the Taliban militia overran the city in the autumn of 1996. The immediate sense of relief that the civil war which had torn the country apart in recent years seemed to be over was soon replaced with a profound sense of unease as reports began to filter out about the Taliban's treatment of women and girls. They were peremptorily excluded from every area of public life: sacked from their jobs, banned from receiving education, evicted from hospitals, and no longer allowed to emerge from their houses or apartments without donning the *burka*, an all-enveloping garment flowing to the ground from a scalp-hugging cap. Television footage and newspaper photographs showed anonymous female figures scurrying home from shopping expeditions, the edges of their veils held nervously together for fear of showing as much as an ankle – an offence guaranteed to result in a beating, if a member of the militia happened to be present to witness it. Even hairdressing salons and beauty parlours were outlawed, condemning the female population to an existence spent in seclusion – a curfew just as shocking, in a city where until a few days before 70 per cent of government employees had been women, as it would be in Paris or London. 'Sitting at home like this, unable to do anything, it's a kind of slow way of killing us,' one woman told the *Independent*. Like other Afghan women, she had been reduced to viewing the world outside her house through the woven mesh mask of her *burka*, like a nun peering through the grille traditionally let into the door of a

Christian convent. At least for nuns, in the late twentieth century, the seclusion is voluntary.

Women in Kabul suddenly looked like entirely different creatures – a different race almost – from men. The Taliban did not just cloister women, they treated them with contempt, expelling eighty female patients from one Kabul hospital and beating up nurses who turned up to look after their patients in another. It was a vivid and unwelcome reminder of how quickly – overnight, in this case – every single human right can be taken away from women, if the regime in power is sufficiently sure of itself. The Taliban's behaviour upset even hardline Muslims in other Islamic countries who, while they seek to justify the veiling of women and their exclusion from public life, go out of their way to stress the respect due to women according to the Koran; even the Iranian government, hardly known for its enlightened treatment of women, publicly condemned the Taliban regime for bringing Islam into disrepute. Yet there is some scriptural authority for the way in which the new government sequestered women, and for their use of physical violence against anyone who rebelled. The Koran says:

Men have authority over women because God has made the one superior to the other, and because they spend their wealth to maintain them. Good women are obedient. They guard their unseen parts because God has guarded them. As for those from whom you fear disobedience, admonish them and send them to beds apart and beat them. Then if they obey you, take no further action against them.

Another passage, interpreted very literally, can be used to justify both the veiling of women and the enforcement of a circumscribed existence within the confines of the extended family:

Enjoin believing women to turn their eyes away from temptation and to preserve their chastity; to cover their adornments (except such as are normally displayed); to draw their veils over their bosoms and not to reveal their finery except to their husbands, their fathers, their husbands' fathers, their sons, their step-sons, their brothers, their brothers' sons, their sisters' sons, their women-servants, and their slave-girls; male attendants lacking in natural vigour, and children who have no carnal knowledge of women. And let them not stamp their feet when walking so as to reveal their hidden trinkets.

It all turns on how you interpret the word 'temptation'. For the Taliban, allowing women to be treated in hospital apparently carried an unacceptable risk that their modesty would be compromised in overcrowded wards. But an *Independent* journalist, reporting from Kabul a few days after the militia took over, suggested that the new government was motivated not just by religious fundamentalism but by an unusually functional view, in this day and age, of the entire female sex. He wrote:

Most Taliban come from Kandahar, a southern city, where homosexuality is accepted practice. Among the platoons of Kandahari warriors it is common to see at least one young boy with a flower or two tucked behind his ear. 'They honestly don't like women. For them, women are just for bearing children', said one Kabul doctor disdainfully.

This report, if true, places the Taliban in the same category as those ancient Athenians who confined women to a part of the house known as the *gynaeceum* where they were expected to spend their time on domestic chores and child-rearing. For the philosopher Plato and his circle, as we know from his *Symposium*, love was an elevated emotion felt almost exclusively by men for other men (or boys) while sex with women was a duty to ensure the continuation of the race. Whether the exponents of this polarised view of the two sexes happen to be fifth-century Greeks or members of a twentieth-century Muslim militia, they are equally mistaken in their estimate of women as morally and intellectually inferior. But they are not alone in acting on a set of beliefs about the female sex which is not only unsubstantiated but collapses when tested empirically. Consider for a moment the hostility of many senior officers in the armed forces on both sides of the Atlantic to the recruitment of women, especially into units which might be called on to play a forward role in combat zones. Their argument – that women cannot kill – is demonstrably untrue but remains one of the most frequently voiced objections to the presence of women in armies, on warships and in military aircraft. After the Gulf War, when the fiercely Islamic government of Saudi Arabia was forced temporarily to relax its strict rules so that female US personnel could drive jeeps on its territory, a former commander of the US Marine Corps fulminated against the gradual progression of women from back-room jobs in the military on to the battlefield. General Robert Barrow said:

> Exposure to danger is not combat. Being shot at, even being killed, is not combat. Combat is finding . . . closing with . . . and killing or capturing the enemy. It's killing. And it's done in an environment that is often as difficult as you can possibly imagine. Extremes of climate. Brutality. Death. Dying. It's . . . uncivilised! And women can't do it! Nor should they even be thought of as doing it. The requirements for strength and endurance render them unable to do it. And I may be old-fashioned, but I think the very nature of women disqualifies them from doing it. Women give life. Sustain life. Nurture life. They don't take it.

This is another example of wishful thinking by men about women, but it is no less influential for that. The number of women who want to play a role in combat zones may be small but it is increasing steadily; at the time General Barrow made his speech, there were already 230,000 women serving in the American armed forces, just over 10 per cent of the total. As is often the case, what is really at stake is a myth: military leaders are accustomed to overcome the taboo against killing other human beings by appealing to a higher good, namely the mothers and children left behind at home. This argument loses its force if women (some of them mothers, which has caused widespread unease in the US military) are visibly present in a war zone, driving tanks and piloting helicopters alongside men. Governments which rule by force, like the Taliban in Kabul, have the option of sending women home, which means that their views on what the female sex can and cannot do are never put to the test; in the West, in the late twentieth century, we are not so easily made invisible. But it is hardly surprising if we sometimes confuse how we are treated – what we are told about ourselves – with what we know about our own natures and capacities.

My second proposition follows naturally from the first, and it is that *theories about difference, frequently supported by religious texts, are used to create the asymmetry whose existence they presuppose*. Try to imagine, for a moment, what it would be like to be a girl growing up under the type of extreme segregationist regime I have described above. Without access to education, with no prospect of a career or paid work, with little experience of the outside world, accustomed to the continual scrutiny of male authority figures, it is all too likely that she will turn out illiterate, ignorant and dependent – thus appearing to justify men's pre-existing beliefs about the inferiority of women. Of course, Islam is far from being alone in enforcing a theory of gender dimorphism to the detriment of women; one of the chief aims of the great world religions, including Christianity and Judaism, is to impose crude distinctions of exactly this sort. For centuries Christian communities organised themselves along lines laid down by St Paul, who stated unequivocally that 'the head of the woman is the man'; when this idea finally began to be challenged during the French Revolution, Christian apologists leapt to defend what they saw as the *natural* relation of the sexes. Infuriated by Mary Wollstonecraft's mildly radical *Vindication of the Rights of Woman*, an English clergyman named Thomas Gisborne wrote an early best-seller entitled *Inquiry into the Duties of the Female Sex*, published in London in 1797. Gisborne's statement of the doctrine of separate spheres for men and women, which was to become one of the guiding principles of Victorian society, is worth quoting at length:

The science of legislation, of jurisprudence, of political economy; the conduct of government in all its executive functions; the abstruse researches of erudition; the inexhaustible depths of philosophy; the acquirements subordinate to navigation; the knowledge indispensable in the wide field of commercial enterprises; the arts of defence, and of attack, by land and sea, which the violence or fraud of unprincipled assailants renders needful; these, and other studies, pursuits and occupations, assigned chiefly or entirely to men, demand the efforts of a mind endued with the powers of close and comprehensive reasoning, and of intense and continued application, in a degree in which they are not requisite for the discharge of the customary offices of female duty. It would therefore seem natural to expect, and experience, I think, confirms the justice of the expectation, that the Giver of all good, after bestowing those powers on men with a liberality proportioned to the existing necessity, would impart them to the female mind with a more sparing hand. It was equally natural to expect, that in the dispensation of other qualities and talents, useful and important to both sexes, but particularly suited to the sphere in which women were intended to move, he would confer the larger portion of his bounty on those who needed it the most. It is accordingly manifest, that, in sprightliness and vivacity, in quickness of perception, in fertility of invention, in powers adapted to unbend the brow of the learned, to refresh the over-laboured faculties of the wise, and to diffuse throughout the family circle the enlivening and endearing smile of cheerfulness, the superiority of the female mind is unrivalled.

Of course, Gisborne had got it precisely the wrong way round, in that his homily is descriptive of the *practical consequences* of imposing a regime of separate spheres, not an account of innate abilities or characteristics; very few women, growing up in England in the late eighteenth century, would have understood the principles of jurisprudence or navigation, but that is solely because they were denied access to them. Obvious as this is to a modern observer, the hundreds of thousands of readers who bought his books accepted his argument at face value because it fitted in with their prejudices. In fact, advice books like Gisborne's were hugely popular throughout the nineteenth century, especially during periods of political unrest when questions about the rights of man accidentally stirred up parallel inquiries about the rights of women. The anonymous author of *Woman's Rights and Duties*, published in London in 1842, insisted it was innate qualities rather than conditioning which made women different from men:

> But whatever the social influences under which women exist, it is everywhere observed of them that they are naturally more tender, compassionate, and gentle than men, and more disinterested; that they are more conscientious, more pious, more contented, and that their temperament is more gay and cheerful; that they have less ambition, are less courageous, active, and enterprising than the other sex, and have less perseverance.

Two years later, however, anxiety was beginning to surface about whether women might be able, after all, to function perfectly well in the public world which had thus far been denied to them. Another anonymous author appealed, like Gisborne, to God as the final arbiter, writing in *Woman's Mission*:

> We claim for [woman] no less an office than that of instruments (under God) for the regeneration of the world – restorers of God's image in the human soul. Can any of the warmest advocates of the political rights of woman claim or assert for her a more exalted mission – a nobler destiny! That she will best accomplish this mission by moving in the sphere which God and nature have appointed, and not by quitting that sphere for another, it is the object of these pages to prove.

In fact, only a couple of decades later, a new scepticism fuelled by Charles Darwin's theory of evolution – the first edition of his *Origin of Species* was published in 1859 – meant that Christianity was losing its force in the West as the definitive court of appeal on the question of the supposed differences between men and women. What happened next gives rise to my third proposition, which is that *there is far more evidence of a craving in all cultures for gender dimorphism than evidence that it actually exists*. In other words, as God's authority waned, along came a new discipline which slowly but certainly developed a novel and influential theory of sex difference. Here is a section from one of its founding texts, first published in 1905 under the unequivocal subheading 'The Differentiation between Men and Women':

> As we all know, it is not until puberty that the sharp distinction is established between the masculine and feminine characters. *From that time on, this contrast has a more decisive influence than any other upon the shaping of human life.* It is true that the masculine and feminine dispositions are already easily recognizable in childhood. The development of the inhibitions of sexuality (shame, disgust, pity, etc) takes place in little girls earlier and in the face of less resistance than in boys; the tendency to sexual repression seems in general to be greater; and, where the component instincts of sexuality appear, they prefer the passive form. [My italics.]

The author is of course Sigmund Freud, and the extract is taken from his *Three Essays on the Theory of Sexuality*. What Freud did, ironically for a non-believer, was fill the vacuum left by God; drawing on a narrow sample of patients – bored and discontented middle-class women who were suffering from that peculiarly late-nineteenth-century female condition, hysteria – he fell into the familiar trap of confusing acquired characteristics with innate attributes. This is not to deny the value of many of his insights, especially on the subject of infantile sexuality, but it is striking that two of his 'discoveries', penis envy and the idea that the libido is always masculine, were not only part of a new theory of gender dimorphism but defined women, at a time when they were agitating across Europe for political and social rights, as men *manqués*. Penis envy in particular, which most twentieth-century women dismiss as a symptom of the *male* obsession with size if they believe in it at all, was a useful means of explaining away the conduct of any woman who did not act in an approved feminine manner. What Freud actually wrote is, in this instance, less important than what he was perceived to have written; for decades women who have attempted to escape gender stereotyping have been accused of wanting to be men.

Freud's influence has waned in recent years, partly because of feminist deconstructions and reinterpretations of his work, but the search for discourses which support the idea of sex difference is as frantic as ever. One route is science, which has prompted hundreds of column inches of stories in which journalists claim that researchers have discovered conclusive evidence of differences between male and female brains – a small-scale American study, for example, which suggested that the hypothalamus is smaller in women (and gay men) than in heterosexual males. What is interesting about these reports, given that few journalists are in a position to assess research published in specialist scientific journals, is the prominence and the interpretation given to them. Here is a classic example from a front-page story in the *Daily Telegraph*: 'It's official: women really do talk more than men' was the headline over a report which claimed that scientists had discovered significant differences in an area of the brain which is associated with language skills. The paper reported excitedly:

> Men are ever happy to agree that women talk too much. But now scientists in Australia have come up with an explanation – the reason may be purely anatomical.
> They have found that specific areas of the brain which control language are larger in women than they are in men.

In fact, two things were striking about the study. Once again, the sample was very small – comparing the brains of only ten men and eleven women – and it was about verbal fluency rather than, as the *Telegraph* suggested, the *amount* of time women spend talking (the word 'gossip', although it did not appear in the story, was implied). In that sense, these reports of preliminary findings, often difficult to interpret and quite possibly contradicted by other research, say more about the longing for concrete proof of gender dimorphism than about whether such differences really exist. More influential, though, than any of these studies are the publications of the self-help movement, the literature of personal growth which has been one of the biggest success stories in publishing, especially in North America, in the last decade. Robert Bly's *Iron John*, which has been credited with founding a men's movement analagous to feminism in the United States, urges men to get out of cities and away from their womenfolk in order to recover their lost masculinity; it offers a nervous theory of gender difference, full of Jungian archetypes, while trying simultaneously not to offend the women – mostly mothers – who are supposedly responsible for its readers' impaired sense of maleness. But the runaway leader in the field is John Gray's *Men Are From Mars, Women Are From Venus* which dominated the *New York Times* best-seller list for months and remained, four years after its British publication, firmly in the paperback top twenty. Its thesis, as implied by the title, is a version of gender dimorphism so extreme that men and women might as well be space aliens trapped in a mutual morass of misunderstanding – a message which has struck a chord, it seems, with millions of readers. This is how Gray summarises his thesis in his introduction:

> So many people are frustrated in their relationships. They love their partners, but when there is tension they do not know what to do to make things better. *Through understanding how completely different men and women are, you will learn new ways for successfully relating with, listening to, and supporting the opposite sex.* You will learn how to create the love you deserve. As you read this book you may wonder how anybody succeeds in having a successful relationship without it.
>
> *Men Are From Mars, Women Are From Venus* is a manual for loving relationships in the 1990s. *It reveals how men and women differ in all areas of their lives.* Not only do men and women communicate differently but they think, feel, perceive, react, respond, love, need, and appreciate differently. They almost seem to be from different planets, speaking different languages and needing different nourishment. [My italics.]

The portrait of the two sexes painted by Gray is a predictable one: men are strong but have trouble communicating their feelings, women get frustrated and try to change their partners. This, according to Gray, is wrong, wrong, wrong. His book is full of warnings to women such as 'any attempt to change [your partner] takes away the loving trust, acceptance, appreciation, admiration, approval, and encouragement that are his primary needs' and 'a man needs to be accepted regardless of his imperfections'. A man's task, in Gray's view, is to learn to listen to his partner; a woman is in the much more onerous business of discovering how to 'empower' her lover or husband. Even in this distinctly New Age universe, being a woman involves giving something up, putting someone else first – a conscious exercise in altruism.

This brings me to my fourth proposition, which is that *being a woman is not just a state but a moral condition*. One of the themes of this book is the extent to which women face tests every day of their lives, whether it is the small one implied in the title of Margaret Forster's novel *Have the Men Had Enough?* (evoking the unwritten rule that a woman's primary role at mealtimes is to make sure her husband and sons are well fed) to major decisions like not returning to work when their children are small or giving up their jobs to look after elderly relatives. We have already seen that nine out of ten single-parent families in Britain are headed by women; while the numbers of men and women looking after a sick or elderly person in their own homes are about equal, women are more likely to care for someone outside their own household, including neighbours. (Predictably, it is married women in the forty-five to sixty-four age group who are most likely to be carers, reflecting the assumption that they will take responsibility for their elderly parents, parents-in-law and other aged relatives.) Women are judged for having too few or too many children, for deciding not to have them at all, for neglecting or spoiling them, for failing to take care of their husbands or partners, for their sexual conduct – where are the male equivalents of 'whore' and 'nymphomaniac'? – for any decision, in other words, which gives the impression they are putting their own needs first. A graphic example of this moral asymmetry was the reporting of the death of the climber Allison Hargreaves, whose decision to leave her husband and children behind in England while she attempted to climb one of the world's most dangerous mountains prompted widespread condemnation in the days after her fatal accident in 1995. Men who die on mountains or in wars – the situation in which men are most likely to face a test of altruism – are heroes, even if they have wives and children; mothers are selfish and foolhardy.

By now, the advantages to men of theories of gender dimorphism, whatever their origin, should be becoming obvious: they highlight female behaviour, setting impossibly high standards and ensuring that it is women's conduct which takes centre stage when it comes to criticism. (This is, I think, the idea behind the feminist aphorism that all women are in some sense female impersonators.) But the narrow boundaries within which a woman has to operate if she is to retain her femininity have another baleful effect, which brings me to my fifth and final proposition. Reflecting the title of this book, it is that *women are expected to be different from men but the same as each other*. What I mean by this is that while there is general agreement that women are unlike men in numerous ill-defined ways, there is enormous reluctance to accept the idea that women might not be broadly similar to each other. The issue which exposes this distinction most sharply is motherhood, so that a woman who chooses not to give birth is characterised not just as unnatural but as a traitor to her sex. Over the years, I have been accused more times than I can remember of insulting women who have children (or who might at some point in the future have children) because of a decision I have taken *about myself*. I have never argued that all women shouldn't have children, just that some do not want to and should not be coerced into involuntary motherhood, yet this entirely reasonable request for tolerance stirs up spectacularly hostile emotions. Of course, the assumption of a bland uniformity among women has insidious effects in other spheres as well; the classic example is when a high-flying City executive announces that she's giving up her job because she can't do it properly and look after her children. Columnists immediately rush into print, crowing that 'you can't have it all' and making working mothers who haven't given up their jobs feel guilty, when the real point is that each woman's circumstances are different and she should be able to decide for herself. When a man gives up politics to spend more time with his family, by contrast, no one suggests that every other male MP should immediately resign his seat and return to the family home.

This brings me to my conclusion, which is that it is time for women to insist on self-definition instead of nervously listening to and absorbing the cultural messages, no matter how strident, which tell us that we have to behave in a certain way or we will no longer be real women. The novelist Dorothy L. Sayers once wrote:

> The first thing that strikes the careless observer is that women are unlike men. They are 'the opposite sex' (though why 'opposite' I do not know; what is the 'neighbouring sex'?) But the fundamental thing is that women are more like men than anything else in the world.

What Sayers did not address is why so many people, particularly those in positions of authority like religious leaders and polticians, have invested so much in the notion that men and women are radically different instead of recognising our common humanity. The answer is that difference, when imposed from the outside, almost always means different-and-inferior rather than different-but-equal; there is an analogy here with race, in that stigmatising the black population as inferior conferred massive material benefits on the white citizens of South Africa during the days of apartheid. The whole point of gender dimorphism, as it has been constructed for centuries, is that it means that someone – almost invariably someone who isn't female – gets to judge what is and isn't acceptable for women. Until very recently indeed, even in the West, women were told what sort of education was appropriate for them, who to marry, whether or not they should work, how many children they should have and how to bring them up, even how to dress. (That, by the way, is why the generation of feminists who became active in the 1960s reacted so violently to the traditional trappings of femininity and acquired a reputation for bra-burning – a gesture which may never have happened but which came to stand for a wider refusal to conform to externally imposed standards of sexiness and beauty. It is one thing to exaggerate secondary sexual characteristics from choice, as many of us do three decades on, and quite another to have it forced on you.) As this book has shown, it is still much harder for women than for men to express themselves as individuals and the penalties for failing to conform remain high – in countries like Algeria, the sanction is sometimes murder.

One of the things that motivated me to write it is a vision of history in which men parade in colourful costumes, unashamedly competing for attention, while women stream past in a more or less undifferentiated mass, with only the occasional individual daring to break ranks: the rest appear as silhouettes. Of course this is a simplification but it does nevertheless contain a truth; in the nineteenth and twentieth centures more women have stepped out of line, but exceptions such as Margaret Thatcher fascinate us precisely because the higher echelons of power are still predominantly masculine terrain. What excites me, however, is trying to imagine what the human race would look like if we abandoned tired old theories which insist that it always has been, and always will be, different for girls. I'm not talking here about the superficial attractions of girl power, as exemplified by the late 1990s phenomenon of the Spice Girls. What I'm suggesting is that boundaries are made to be broken, and that some of us are already beginning to discover the scary but thrilling consequences of throwing off other people's expectations and declaring ourselves self-made women.

Notes

Introduction

ix   'Assertive women': *Guardian*, 16 April 1996.
     'Official: men finally losing': *Sunday Times*, 5 May 1996.
     'Taller and wider women': *Sunday Telegraph*, 21 July 1996.
x   'The gap between the sexes': *Daily Telegraph*, 25 July 1996.

To Di For: the Queen of Broken Hearts

4   'US dazzled': *Daily Telegraph*, 26 September 1996.
4   'Princess Diana': *Hello!* 5 October 1996.
5   'The New Diana': *Majesty*, vol. 17, no. 9.
       'the Princess believes': *Royalty*, vol. 14, no. 5.
       'She was dressed': Charles Dickens, *Great Expectations*, 1860–1
       Penguin edition, p.87.
8   'Do you know': ibid., p.88.
10   'I knew I had to': Andrew Morton, *Diana, Her True Story*,
       Michael O'Mara, 1992, p.44.
11   'Broken: Fergie's final shame': *Sun*, 4 October 1996.
12–13 All quotes from Morton.
14   'The night before the wedding': ibid., p.65.
       'While a small voice': ibid., p.5.
15   'She could hear': ibid., p.9.
16   'It was not': *Great Expectations*, p.87.

19   *Little Women*, Louisa M. Alcott, 1868; Puffin, p.282.
21   The number of divorces in Britain: *Guardian Weekend*, 8 July
         1995, p.15.
21–23   all newspaper quotations: ibid.
23   typical issue of Brides magazine: *Brides and Setting Up Home*,
         Sept./Oct. 1996.
26   'Her person': Lawrence Stone, *Road to Divorce: A History
         of the Making and Breaking of Marriage in England*, OUP,
         1990, p.13.
26–27   all cases cited: ibid.
27   'Everything has its appointed': (Rev. Daniel Wise, *The Young
         Lady's Counsellor, or Outlines and Illustrations of the Sphere,
         the Duties, and the Dangers of Young Women*, Carlton &
         Porter, 1851, pp.91–2.
28–29   Mrs Belcher: Stone, p.204.
31   almost a third of babies: *Guardian*, 30 May 1996.

The Last Silent Movie Star

33   The first item: *Daily Telegraph*, 24 April 1996.
         'It's incredible' *Guardian*, 25 April 1996.
34   In the Middle Ages: see Catherine Walker Bynum, *Holy Feast
         and Holy Fast: The Religious Significance of Food to Mediaeval
         Women*, University of California Press, 1987.
35   'Three hours later': Giuseppe Tomasi di Lampedusa, *The Leop-
         ard*, 1958, trans. Archibald Colquhoun.
37   'So the epitaph': C. David Heymann, *A Woman Named Jackie*,
         Mandarin, 1989 p.419.
         'Book takes shine off': *Guardian*, 8 August 1996.
38   'Queen Deb of the year': Susan Marvin, *The Women Around
         RFK*, Lancer Books, 1967, p.48.
39   'Janet told Jackie': *Vanity Fair*, September 1996, p.152.
40   'When Jacqueline, Kennedy': Marvin, p.57.
41   'Among the items': ibid., p.65.
43   'We finally reached': Heymann, pp.551–2.
44   'a Southern routine': ibid., p.81.
46–47   the filmed biography: *Guardian*, 31 August 1996.

49   the extremely low success rate: *Guardian*, 23 November 1996.

51   Professor Jack Scarisbrick: *Guardian*, 4 December 1996.

52   'Mandy needs a miracle now': *Evening Standard*, 1 October 1996.
Credo of the People of God: *Catechism of the Catholic Church*, Geoffrey Chapman, 1994, p.223.

53   'And the angel': Luke I: 28–38.

54   litany of Loreto: Marina Warner, *Monuments and Maidens*, Weidenfeld & Nicolson, 1985, p.254.
The word 'bag': Jane Mills, *Womanwords*, Longman, 1989, p.16.
'A woman is the weaker': Anthony Fletcher, *Gender, Sex and Subordination in England 1500–1800*, Yale University Press, 1995, p.60.

55   the uterus as: *ibid*. p.64.
'longs to generate': Mills, p.123.

56   'So artificially formed': Fletcher, p.64.
'If women get tired': Mills, p.168.

57   a 58-year-old London woman: *Guardian*, 16 August 1993.

58   Professor Ian Craft: *Life* magazine, *Observer*, 4 June 1995, p.16.
Professor Richard Lilford: *Guardian*, 16 August 1993.

59   'even those patients': Maureen Freely and Celia Pyper, *Pandora's Clock*, Heinemann, 1993, p.87.
A brain-dead woman: *Guardian*, 16 August 1993.
Sarah Mapes: *Cosmopolitan*, November 1996, p.45.

59–60   Doctors break the news: *ibid*., p.45.

61   'It seems so simple': *ibid*., p.46.

I'm Gonna Make You A ...

64   'so much a forerunner': Lyndall Gordon, *Charlotte Brontë: A Passionate Life*, Chatto & Windus, 1994, p.187.

65   'a woman's face': Jan Marsh, *Pre-Raphaelite Sisterhood*, Quartet, 1985, p.1.

66   'At another level': ibid.

67   'without even the habits': ibid., p.60.

68   'a misshapen German Jew:' ibid. p.326.
      'What a stupendously': ibid., p.16.
69   'You look really good': Michael Gross, *Model: The Ugly Business of Beautiful Women*, Bantam, 1995, p.408.
70   'I'm going to make': ibid., p.416.
      Aline Wermelinger: ibid., pp.427–8.
      'That's how [Schiffer]' ibid., p.418.
71   public dressing-down: *Guardian*, 15 October 1996.
72   ludicrous black wig: *Daily Telegraph*, 15 October 1996.
73   'While [McQueen] is certainly': *Guardian*, 15 October 1996.
74   'Without him knowing it': ibid.

The Selfish Jean

79   In Austria, Belgium: statistics on birth rates and populations are taken from Huw Jones, *Population Geography*, Paul Chapman Publishing, second edition, 1990.
80   Their plight: details of the marriage of Francesco di Marco Datini and Margherita di Domenico Bandini are taken from Iris Origo, *The Merchant of Prato* (1957); Penguin edition, 1963.
81   'She says it is': ibid., p.163.
      'A family': Marie Stopes, *Wise Parenthood*, G. P. Putnam's Sons, 1918, p.1.
82   'Although our culture': Boston Women's Health Book Collective, *Our Bodies Ourselves*, 1971; British edition, Penguin, 1978, p.344.
      Judith Arcana: Judith Arcana, *Our Mother's Daughters*, Women's Press, 1981, p.181.
      Ellen Peck: Ellen Peck, *The Baby Trap*, Heinrich Hanau, 1973.
      The figure had always been: figures taken from *Social Focus on Women*, HMSO, 1995, p.16.
83   A front-page article: *Guardian*, 14 June 1996.
84   The earth's population: figures taken from Jones.
      'The raging monster': Edward O. Wilson, *The Diversity of Life*, Penguin, 1992, p.314.
85   'Technological advances': Jones, p.260.
87   'The thing that': *Independent*, 11 July 1996.
89   St Catherine of Siena: details of Catherine's life are taken from

Caroline Walker Bynum, *Holy Feast and Holy Fast*, University of California Press, 1987.

90   'Why Are Women Redundant': quoted in Elaine Showalter, *Sexual Anarchy*, Bloomsbury, 1990, p.19.

91   'How to Provide': ibid., p.20.

The Lady Vanishes

94   'has modern characters': Pauline Kael, *Taking It All In: Film Writings 1980–1983*, Arena, 1987, pp.256–7.

96   In this version: James M. Cain, *Double Indemnity* (1945); Pan edition, p.120.

101   Jacques Lacan: quoted in Darian Leader, *Why Do Women Write More Letters Than They Post*, Faber, 1996, p.89.

Single, White, Fertile

103   'Paula: I'll fight': *Evening Standard*, 1 October 1996.

104   'I've always tried': Paula Yates, *The Autobiography*, Thorsons, 1995, p.140.

105   'Bob said': ibid., p.125.
       'Pregnant at 15': *Daily Mail*, 22 July 1996.
       'Up to 40 per cent': *Sunday Telegraph*, 1 December 1996.

106   'Spare the job': *Sunday Telegraph*, 27 October 1996.

107   'Working mums are blamed': *Guardian*, 3 February 1997.

108   'Children of working mothers': *Sunday Times*, 2 February 1997.
       'There isn't a scrap': *Daily Telegraph*, 4 February 1997.
       'There is no evidence': *Observer*, 9 February 1997.

109   'I have been': *Daily Telegraph*, 4 February 1997.

111   'Jobs drive': *Guardian*, 6 February 1997.
       'Children raised by': quoted in *Newsweek*, 20 January 1997, p.45.

112   around £8 *billion*: *Guardian*, 6 February 1997.
       the government's own statistics: *Social Focus on Women*, HMSO, 1995, p.18.

112 'to replace a child maintenance': *Child Support Agency Annual Report and Accounts 1995/96*, HMSO, p.5.

113 the CSA's live caseload: figure from CSA press office, 13 February 1997.
no absent parent: *CSA Annual Report*, pp.10 and 76.
it undertook more: ibid., p.12.
'In many of these cases': ibid.
95.2 per cent: figure from CSA press office, 13 February 1997.

114 since the introduction: *CSA Annual Report*, p.13.

115 'One in three British babies': *Independent on Sunday*, 24 November 1996.

The Love That Dare Not Speak Its Name

119–25 An article in: all quotations taken from John De St Jorre, 'The
119 Unmasking of O', *New Yorker*, 1 August 1994.

121 'Seeing herself': Pauline Réage, *The Story of O*, (1954); Corgi edition p.263.
'Here we have it': Jean Paulhan, 'A Slave's Revolt', in ibid., p.272.

125 'The line raced': Virginia Woolf, 'Professions for Women', 1931. collected in *Women and Writing*, Women's Press, pp.61–62.

126 'Why have British women writers': *Daily Mail*, 22 May 1996.

127 'Frannie is a woman': *Observer*, 28 April 1996.

128 'Do you know': ibid.

129 'Although the superstar': *Daily Mail*, 14 February 1996.

130 'Madonna is gaining': *Daily Mail*, 2 November 1995.

Unnatural Born Killers

133–35 All quotations are from newspapers published in the final week of Rosemary West's trial. She was convicted and sentenced at Winchester Crown Court on 22 November 1995.

135 a book about the Moors murders: Robert Wilson, *Devil's Disciples*, Javelin Books, 1986, p.96.

136   'There are no known cases': quoted in Jane Caputi, *The Age of Sex Crime*, Women's Press, 1987, p.203 n. 6.

137   Charles McCabe: for a fuller discussion of responses to Jack the Ripper see ibid., pp.14–17.
       'Why do we get': David Canter, *Criminal Shadows*, Harper-Collins, 1994, p.217.
       the numbers of serial killers: figures taken from Caputi, pp.1–2.

138   'West's wife may go free': *Evening Standard*, 3 January 1995.

139   Frederick West's suicide: for a fuller discussion of contradictions in the case against Rosemary West, see Brian Masters, *'She Must Have Known': The Trial of Rosemary West*, Doubleday, 1996.

140   'Typically in these events': this and further quotes from David Canter taken from press agency interview, November 1995.
       'On the few occasions': Helena Kennedy, *Eve Was Framed: Women and British Justice*, Chatto & Windus, 1992, p.249.

141   'In two of the single female': Emlyn Williams, *Beyond Belief*, 1967; Pan edition, p.159.

145   'Some women': Kennedy, p.249.
       'She cannot accuse me': Emily Brontë, *Wuthering Heights* (1847); Penguin edition, p.149.

146   'I Rose': Masters, p.128.
       The other: ibid., pp.128–9.
       'is the vessel': Kennedy, p.242.

Five Propositions and a Conclusion

151   'conditioning usually reinforces': Matt Ridley, *The Red Queen*, Penguin, 1993, p.172.

152   'Even among the most liberated': ibid.

154–55 A much more dramatic: details of the Taliban regime in Kabul are taken from 'The Veil of Tears', a report by Tim McGirk in the *Independent*, 9 October 1996.

155   'Men have authority': the Koran, translated by N.J. Dawood, revised edition, Penguin, 1995, p.64.
       'Enjoin believing women': ibid: p.248.

156   'Most Taliban': McGirk, ibid.

157   'Exposure to danger': quoted in Kate Muir, *Arms and the Woman*, Sinclair-Stevenson, 1992, pp.2–3.

161   'As we all know': Sigmund Freud, The Pelican Freud Library, vol. 8: *On Sexuality*, p.141.

162   'Men are ever happy': *Daily Telegraph*, 24 February 1997.

163   'So many people': John Gray, *Men Are From Mars, Women Are From Venus*, Thorsons, 1992, p.5.

164   Predictably, it is married women: *Social Focus on Women*, HMSO, 1995, p.19.

166   'The first thing': quoted in Thomas Laqueur, *Making Sex: Body and Gender from the Greeks to Freud*, Harvard University Press, 1990, p.1.